# ENDORSEMENTS

Get ready for a unique journey with Matt Weaver in his book, *The E2 Factor*. From the beginning Matt's creativity and storytelling breaks away from a book simply on economics. Suddenly you are following a carefully outlined path into the Kingdom and how to come into the realms of fullness. You are going to love this book and the challenge to walk in personal favor and into a place of influence and abundance. You will learn how the Lord blesses and flows through you to release His heart and overflowing love. This book will saturate you with the knowledge that you genuinely carry and impart the kingdom of heaven on earth.

**MARK TUBBS**
Founder "Transformation of the Nations"
Harvest International Ministry Missions Apostle

I want to express my sincere gratitude to Matt Weaver for such an excellent and timely word. *The E2 Factor: Ekklesia, Economics and the Prosperous House of God* clearly lays out the Kingdom plan of our Heavenly Father that we are destined to function as His chief stewards. We are those who align with His divine strategy of innovation and wealth creation to be the Kingdom ambassadors in every realm of society. Learn how to break out of a poverty spirit empowered by fear and into Kingdom identity, blessing, favor, expectation, belief, and abundance. Now is the time for the Ekklesia to arise with strategies to defeat systemic poverty and to see the transfer of wealth. As Matt eloquently states, "As disciples of Christ and influencers in the world, we must experience Kingdom-of-God economics and stewardship if we are to gain credibility to invite the nations into an encounter with the King." This book is a must read for every believer who has a passion to see true Kingdom transformation.

**Rebecca Greenwood**
Cofounder
Christian Harvest International, Strategic Prayer Apostolic Network
International Freedom Group
Christian Harvest Training Center

Now more than ever, the world is desperate for answers. Nations are being shaken, uncertainty is widespread, and economies are facing an unprecedented season of crisis. It is "for such a time as this" that God says, "I will shake all the nations; and they will come with the wealth of all nations, and I will fill this house with glory" (Haggai 2:7).

In this extraordinary chapter in history, my friend Matthew Weaver has written a timely book that will equip believers to navigate economics with a refreshing biblical perspective. *The E2 Factor* is full of stories of God's provision and truths that will impact the way you steward your resources. You will discover that the Body of Christ truly is called to lead our lives operating from the economy of God's Kingdom, as we expand heaven's reach into our spheres of influence. We are part of an eternal Kingdom that cannot be shaken. I believe it is time for the Church to rise up and shine the glory of God across the nations of the earth—to see transformation of lives, communities, and entire economies.

**DR. CHÉ AHN**
Founder and President, Harvest International Ministry
Founding and Senior Pastor, Harvest Rock Church, Pasadena, CA
International Chancellor, Wagner University
Founder, Ché Ahn Ministries

# THE E2 FACTOR

## Ekklesia, Economics,
## and the Prosperous House of God

## MATTHEW L. WEAVER

outskirts
press

# Acknowledgments

Measuring the immeasurable is worth the effort. It seems impossible to adequately show my thanks to so many who have encouraged, supported, and launched me in the writing of this book. Nonetheless, to all of you I give you my deepest gratitude.

To my wife, Lisa, I owe the greatest measure of thanks. You have encouraged me to pursue this work for years. I value our partnership in every aspect of our lives—a rich family, wonderful church, and fabulous business. Your expertise and wisdom in helping to edit this book has been so valuable. And you have taught me so much about life as a mature son and a wise steward. I love walking with you.

And my life is so blessed by my children, Shandra, Katie, Scott, and Audrey. When I learned how to be a good son, I discovered how much I loved being a father. Thank you for enriching my life. And how much I love being Papa to those unbelievably cute granddaughters!

To the people of The River Ekklesia, thank you for supporting me in the process of writing this book and pursuing my doctoral degree. What an amazing gathering of people. I cannot think of a better collection of warriors, worshipers, and servants to bring transformational impact to our region.

I have been blessed these last few years to find encouragement and support from Dr. Che and Sue Ahn. Alignment with you as our apostle in Harvest International Ministries and Wagner University have provided a stream of grace allowing us access to places we never dreamed we could go. Your confidence in us inspires us for the manifestation of the Kingdom in the Treasure State.

Mark and Ann Tubbs, with Transformation of the Nations—I would go anywhere with you. Your apostolic and prophetic guidance has been invaluable to Lisa and me. Your revelation of the five-fold has given me relational context for writing this book. You have served us well as chief stewards, providing us with the right food at the right time.

And to Wagner University, I am deeply grateful. Dr. Benny Yang, Dr. Dave Collins, and Dr. Greg Wallace, you have challenged me to go higher, dig deeper, and steward well the resources God has made available to us. Your trust and encouragement have stimulated me to pursue excellence in spirit as well as Kingdom academics. While this book is written in fulfillment of my doctoral degree for Wagner University, some of its content can be found in seed form in Chapter 9 of Wagner University's book by Cohort 1807, *My Father's Business: Discipling Nations*, "Heaven's economy."[1]

And finally, to our clients and many friends and family who have taught us how to prosper in soul, may God set all of you on a good path and prosper each of you in all of life.

# Table of Contents

Introduction: Blueprint for Building the Prosperous House of God.....i

Preface: The Caretaker.................................................................ix

1. Seeking First the Kingdom .....................................................1
2. Glory and the Economy of Heaven.......................................10
3. Stewards of the House of God...............................................22
4. God's Extravagant Economy.................................................34
5. The Economy of Grace..........................................................47
6. The Art of Distribution.........................................................59
7. Economic Warfare.................................................................73
8. You Look Just Like Your Dad...............................................88
9. Chief Oikonomos................................................................101
10. Economics in the "Real World"...........................................112
11. Wealth Transfer and Kingdom Advancement .....................125
12. Living in Heaven on Earth .................................................141

Bibliography ...........................................................................151
Endnotes .................................................................................157

# Introduction:
# Blueprint for Building the
# Prosperous House of God

Rich deposits of truth are buried within the puzzling landscape of economics. But invite people into conversations about economics, and they stumble over themselves to avoid the rugged terrain. Throw in words like "tithe," "stewardship," and "prosperity" and you would think you were inviting them to walk through treacherous land mines and exploding geysers.

Every kingdom has an economy. Even the Kingdom of God. Jesus invited his disciples to pray with expectation, "Your kingdom come, your will be done, on earth as it is in heaven" (Matthew 6:10). The request pulls the reality of heaven into earth. Heaven's "already" meets earth's "not yet" and a "suddenly" is born. A young boy's lunch feeds thousands. A fisherman throws his empty net to the other side of the boat and needs help hauling his economic windfall. These "suddenlies" are powerful economic forces in the brilliant display of the Kingdom of God.

Leaders in every realm of influence grapple with economic realities. We expect that of business and governmental leaders, of course. But every educator, artist, church leader, head of household, or media director is confronted by difficult decisions. Excellence may be the stated value, but all of us know how the lack of money severely limits our ability to reach our goals and vision.

In the Church's realm of influence, religion has constructed a rut with confusing values. Poverty is touted as a virtue. We are taught, "The poor are blessed, the wealthy are cursed." On the other hand, prosperity theology in the mouths of the immature flirts around the gate of greed. Talk too much about finances and you are a money-hungry ministry. But say nothing and the bills don't get paid. Because the Church is confused about economics, Christian leaders in every other realm of authority lack resources and credibility in bringing transformation to their region of influence.

In the realm of Church in America, 3 to 5 percent of churchgoers are tithers. Of Protestants in the U.S., average giving is $17 per week, and 37 percent of all regular church attendees, including Evangelicals, do not give any money at all.[2] According to the National Association of Evangelicals in 2017, 50 percent of pastors made less than $50,000, 62 percent had no retirement, and 59 percent had no health insurance. Christians in the U.S. in 2017 gave 2.5 percent of their income to the church; during the Great Depression they gave 3.3 percent.[3] These anecdotal statistics reflect the confusion and powerlessness in the Church concerning money.

How do Christian leaders navigate the tricky waters of religion's value rut, economic pressures, and cultural and political confusion? Is it possible to live NOW in the economy of heaven? What does the King value? How do we live in His economy, aligning with His standards of value?

Our mandate is to "make disciples of all nations" (Matthew 28:19). As disciples of Christ and influencers in the world, we must experience Kingdom-of-God economics and stewardship if we are to gain credibility to invite the nations into an encounter with the King.

The E2 Factor provides Kingdom leaders in the Ekklesia (the first "E-Factor") a practical theological and biblical foundation to bring prosperity in Economy (the second "E-Factor"). Ekklesia and Economy together are exponentially more powerful. Divine prosperity in business or ministry or nations of the earth happen under the favor of God when the Ekklesia operates in the truth of Kingdom Economy. The E2 Factor is unleashed when the Ekklesia operates according to Kingdom principles and accesses the Economic treasures of the Kingdom of Heaven.

By occupation I am a pastor and church planter. I am also a businessman and entrepreneur. This business has allowed me to serve as "chief steward" for numerous successful leaders. I also view much of life through my roles as a father and an apostle. What I enjoy most is engaging others in a journey toward maturity and transformation. As the Ekklesia, we are poised in a perfect season of opportunity to mature in our operation within Kingdom economics and stewardship to bring transformation to our world.

My intent in the *E2 Factor* is to provide vision and tools and language for leaders in ministries, businesses, and other areas of influence to live in the economy of heaven—now, not later. From the foundation of our identity as mature sons and daughters of God, this book is about an expansive definition of the House of God and the keys that we carry for access into the nations of the earth. The paradigms carry power to unlock creativity and innovation in our stewardship of the resources of the King to bring transformation to the nations—and to your business, ministry, and city.

Into each chapter of the *E2 Factor* are woven concepts, principles, scriptures, and stories designed to awaken your inner explorer. This book is a treasure hunt for those looking for valuable things in unlikely places. The terrain we tread every day is littered by the enemy with minefields and traps, a sure indication that truth-treasures are hidden in the field. Scattered throughout this book are vignettes that illustrate my experiences as a maturing son and steward. They are intended as an encouragement to you to engage your imagination to pursue Wisdom in the depths of God's Word and the atmosphere of Holy Spirit.

For those who prefer an overview, a broad sketch of the chapters may draw you to the places where you need to focus to maximize your growth and effectiveness.

**Chapter 1—Ekklesia Seeks the Kingdom First.** Beliefs and assumptions impact our experiences, including our economic realities. The good news is that God has a great way of showing Himself and raising our vision out of impoverished thinking. Christians are beginning to see themselves as the powerful Ekklesia, legislating in God's Kingdom. No longer content to hide in anonymity and poverty, Christians operate with authority and intentionality to impact and transform everything we touch. The church has been reluctant to accept "power" in her language and experience, but as she "seeks first the kingdom of God and righteousness," the King of the domain of all creation is drawing them into His heart and His provision.

**Chapter 2—Glory and the Economy of Heaven.** The foundation of earth's economics is in the surpassing reality of the Kingdom of God. The fact that "God is Love" delivers practical economic outcomes. His heart is the economic engine of heaven. His economy reveals His glory, and glory ignites earth's economy. As the Ekklesia, the children of God are given access to the Father's House. They possess the keys of the Kingdom, not to get into the House, but to release power and resources of the Kingdom into territories long held by the enemy and requiring transformation. God intends that the Ekklesia pull heaven's reality into manifest experience on earth. God's glory covers the earth, and it is the responsibility and privilege of stewards to use Kingdom keys to make it visible. Economics on earth has become the dominant expression of power and influence among the nations. Defining economics is surprisingly easy. The drivers of economics in the earth—the search for fulfillment, purpose, or power—are much more difficult to explain.

**Chapter 3—Stewards of the House.** The Bible chronicles God's intent to build His magnificent House on the earth. His House stewards, administrators of the resources of His estate, are not slaves. They are sons and daughters raised up into maturity and passion *to create value* in the estate rather than simply *maintaining* the House out of duty and fear.

**Chapter 4—God's Extravagant Economy.** The Kingdom of God

has a God-sized economy with massive production capacity, distribution, and consumers with the need for all that God supplies. This vast and endless economy operates in agreement with the nature and purposes of God. The nations of the earth can be awakened through demonstrations of the reality of God's extravagant economy.

**Chapter 5—The Economy of Grace.** Grace is more than an undeserved ticket to access the Almighty. Grace is God's empowerment to reign in life. With one succinct sentence, the apostle Peter provides us a handful of keys to the prosperous economy of God. Each key releases an encounter with God's power and glory. As empowered and gifted administrators, we discover the sweet spot of operating in our measure of strengths, our metron. Administrating heaven's resources releases a strong economy on earth.

**Chapter 6—The Art of Distribution.** The Ekklesia operates as distributors of powerful resources from heaven. These resources are created by God to be supernaturally fruitful. This "Oikonomos Pipeline" is connected both to heaven and to earth. As the Ekklesia distributes these resources, exponential prosperity is available to our businesses and ministries.

**Chapter 7—Economic Warfare.** A usurping enemy actively opposes the House of God and its economy. If we want to win the battles, we must understand our enemy and his methods of attacking and undermining prosperity in God's estate. Wise stewards learn to fight like warriors. Find effective means of protecting your leadership and management teams from division, ineffectiveness, and unproductive practices that war against prosperity. The enemy specializes in subversive tactics, using interdicts to cut off supply lines. But Holy Spirit gives us strategies to break through and flourish.

**Chapter 8—You Look Just Like Your Dad.** Godly character is forged in challenging experiences. When we invite God to the process, we are transformed into authentic, wise stewards. In God's economy, we discover that He provides economic multipliers in experiences we tend to avoid. Even suffering can unlock a multiplying factor in what God wants to produce in us, our ministry, business, or workplace. Our character opens and closes doors and can result in poverty or prosperity. Economists who are faithful with little are given much.

**Chapter 9—Chief Oikonomos.** Leaders are chief stewards. Not everyone can carry the weight of responsibility given to these mature sons and daughters of the Owner of the vast estate of creation. Effective leaders fulfill specific requirements. They enable us to multiply our effectiveness as wise builders of the House of God and the Kingdom economy.

**Chapter 10—Economics in the Real World.** The Ekklesia operates in a real world with desperate needs and obvious deficiencies. The challenges require the Church to break free from slavery to mammon and toil and into heaven-breathed solutions. A true, biblical worldview gives purpose and meaning to creation, and provides a basis for hope to find creative and innovative solutions for earth's devastating problems.

**Chapter 11—Wealth Transfer and Kingdom Advancement.** Making "disciples of all nations" requires building the Kingdom of God, the essence of transformation. The Ekklesia is building powerful structures of glory. Wealth is required to finance the advancement of Kingdom transformation. Generating wealth to transform and disciple people, cities, and nations requires wisdom and active engagement. Wise stewards develop a keen eye for return on investment. Obstacles can be overcome, and preparations can be made for wealth transfer.

**Chapter 12—Living in Heaven on Earth.** Chief stewards are impact leaders on the earth. They release Kingdom authority and resources with their decisions. Dreams, vision, and strategy pull heaven into earth's realm. With the power of expectation, we operate in the principle of Maximum Kingdom Impact. Systems and nations are transformed by the Ekklesia operating in supernatural economics, and the vast Estate of God prospers.

Wisdom is never theoretical. It is truth applied. Knowledge and understanding beg for an outlet, just as surely as a lake needs a stream. Some of what you read may require a level of pondering, meditation, and application. Otherwise, the truths will remain simply theoretical, a "Dead Sea" of religious knowledge with potential but bearing no fruit. Take time to allow God to impart truth to your spirit. If you are tempted to consume the material as head knowledge only, invite Holy Spirit to come alongside and help you.

Paul's doxology, or "word of glory," in Romans 11:33-36 invites us into the Kingdom terrain of economics:

> *Oh, the depth of the riches of the wisdom and knowledge of God!*
> *How unsearchable His judgments, and His paths beyond tracing out!*
> *Who has known the mind of the Lord?*
> *Or who has been His counselor?*
> *Who has ever given to God, that God should repay him?*
> *For from Him and through Him and to Him are all things.*
> *To Him be the glory forever! Amen.*

Your journey into the depths of the riches of the heart of God will release treasures within you. May these pages encourage and stimulate you to explore territory Father has long waited to reveal. And may this book launch you from a strong foundation of truth into a lifelong pursuit of the King and His Kingdom.

Matt Weaver
Bozeman, Montana

# Preface:
# The Caretaker

I stood alone at the edge of the deck. The sun had set, but I hadn't noticed. Weary hearts have a way of dimming the eye. I was dead to horizons. The world turned its back on me and slipped into darkness. Thick shadows shrouded me, the wind threw its chill, but all I could feel was the weight of responsibility and the shame of failure.

Scathing accusations pierced me: "Are you enough? Do you have what it takes? Who do you think you are? You're a fraud." The internal assault bled out what little confidence was left. Standing on the deck, I had no fight, no defense. Not even the heart to run.

I remembered the opening lines of Edwin Markham's poem, "The Man with the Hoe." I memorized it when I was in fifth grade, Mrs. Martel's class. Perhaps the stark painting that accompanied the poem initially drew me to the poem. It looked like an old, haggard peasant trying to rest, but in my eleven-year-old mind I didn't think he could. Maybe because he was surrounded by hard, rocky ground that went on forever. Of course, for a kid stuck in Monday, forever is all the way to Friday.

The words gripped my imagination.
"Bowed by the weight of centuries he leans
Upon his hoe and gazes on the ground,
The emptiness of ages in his face,

*And on his back the burden of the world.*
*Who made him dead to rapture and despair,*
*A thing that grieves not and that never hopes?"[4]*

My small hands felt the tool under a blistering sun, rock after rock impeding progress. Row after row, day after day, century upon century, the relentless pounding and probing of the soil came from deep inside of me. I felt everything around me demanding from me, stealing something; I didn't know what. Stooping was normal. It was all a part of the job.

Forever gets bigger the older you get. So does the job.

When my world went dark, it wasn't the deck I felt beneath my feet. It was my barren field, all the way to my unseen horizon. Day after day, my field didn't just need me, it demanded me. Work like a madman. Keep my head down. God may have created things to grow, but the burden of all of it piles up on my shoulders. Must this infernal plowing, planting, and meager harvest go on to the furthest horizon of my life?

My youthful dreams were fragile wisps in the distance. I was afraid that if I looked at them now, they would disappear completely. Perhaps it would be best if they did. At least they wouldn't show up at the worst times to mock me. Is vision even possible? Is hope so fragile? Is this all that there is?

I shivered in the cold and snapped my head around. The movement helped. It was like slamming a lid to a strongbox of toxic memories and questions. Time for the pastor to get back to work.

# 1

## Seeking First the Kingdom

His generosity overwhelmed us.

Entirely unexpected, pushing against the walls of my limited understanding, He pierced my self-sufficiency and pride, and gave. Lavishly.

In 1987, Lisa, my bride of four years, our newly born daughter, and I moved from Alaska to "the lower forty-eight" to continue my education and serve in an associate position in a church of about a hundred and fifty. A larger church in a nearby community asked us to assist them on weekday evenings with janitorial duties that included their large daycare. I figured I cleaned over a hundred toilets a week.

The nights were late and the work demanding. By day, I was constantly writing papers and attending classes. We coped with issues common to pastors. On top of it all, I was learning how to be a husband and a father. It all combined to make a challenging season.

Adding to the stress was the reality of our household economics. Just as we moved from Alaska, oil prices plummeted. Selling our condominium was virtually impossible if we wanted to recoup our costs. In a matter of three months, its value sank 70 percent. We rented out the property, but the small income fell far short of making the mortgage payment. In hopes of a quick economic turnaround, we sought to make up the difference out of our small salary. We had ten dollars a week remaining for food, diapers, sundries, and clothing.

I plodded along, numbly accepting the burden as "the price you have to pay" for a life of professional ministry. My wife, on the other hand, was feeling the pull of Holy Spirit. A year earlier, while we were still in Alaska, Lisa felt prompted by God to memorize Matthew 6:25-34. Part of the scripture says, "So do not worry, saying, 'What shall we eat?' or 'What shall we drink?' or 'What shall we wear?' For the pagans run after all these things, and your heavenly Father knows that you need them. But seek first His kingdom and His righteousness, and all these things will be given to you as well. Therefore do not worry about tomorrow, for tomorrow will worry about itself. Each day has enough trouble of its own" (Matthew 6:25-34).

The Word worked into her spirit for months. Like a roast in the Crockpot with water and spices and vegetables, the more the heat works into the meat, the more its flavor saturates everything within.

"Your heavenly Father already knows what you need." She heard and trusted His voice, and the heat of our circumstances kept rising. "Seek FIRST the Kingdom of God..." began to release its flavor.

One day while I was in classes and she was in our little duplex, Lisa had an encounter at the kitchen table. It was like the timer went off, the truth-feast was ready, and the Chef came to the table. With her heart and soul marinated in the Word and the fire of our circumstances, she came before Him to seek Him first. With the tenderness of a daughter and the boldness of an intercessor, she cried out, "You SAID that You already know what we need. Father, enough is enough! How is this just? Is it right that we should pay our debts, give You our tithe, and we go hungry? We do not have the essentials, God! Father, You SAID that You would supply ALL our needs. Our baby girl needs food and diapers, God. Father, we love You! Our hearts are for You. You said the righteous would never beg for bread! I'm not going to beg, but I will remind You of Your promises."

She wiped her tears and took a breath. (Every truth encounter needs a Selah.) The great thing about taking a breath is that in the brief silence, there is opportunity to hear God speak. In that breath, Lisa heard God speak.

"Make a list."

With pen and paper at the kitchen table, Lisa began making a list of everything we needed, including soap and toilet paper, baby supplies, groceries, even meat—something recently lacking in our diet. She finished her extensive shopping list, presented it to Father, said thanks, and tucked it away.

Four days later we arrived at the church facility for another Sabbath.

In the auditorium were three tables loaded with vegetables, flour, diapers, meat, even toilet paper. Bags of groceries were overflowing the tables and piling up on the floor. *It was for us.* I was stunned. Lisa wept. She pulled the list she had made from her Bible, the first I knew of it, and unfolded it for me to see. Now both of us wept, unashamed.

Everything from Lisa's list was there—and even more variety than she had requested. It was exceedingly, abundantly beyond what we asked for. Our hearts were overwhelmed and grateful for our Father's compassion and generosity toward us, and for our friends who gave out of their own need or abundance.

There was only one thing missing. She discovered it the next day while going through her list. "Father, thank You for all of this! Everything is here but the laundry soap. How do You want to provide that?" There was a quick rap on the door. Lisa opened it to discover a packaged sample of laundry soap. God's wink. Truth encounter established. She sought Him first and according to His word. All the things we needed were added to us!

Lisa and I experienced an amazing outpouring of provision from God and our friends at a crucial time in our lives. This became a foundation for transformation.

So why did we continue living our lives on the edge of burnout, borderline impoverishment, and powerlessness? That is a great question.

We had been taught that we were trapped in a broken world. Because of Adam's sin we accepted the devastating news that we were doomed to a life of toil. So we never bothered to lift our heads and behold the glorious economy of heaven that had been opened to us through the cross and resurrection. God bombarded our fortress of lack with lavish demonstrations of His infinite provision.

Over the next decade, Father repeatedly encountered us with His kindness. He provided a vehicle when ours had been vandalized; winter coats when we moved to a colder climate; Christmas gifts when we had no money...the list goes on. Yet our core belief system was slow to change. Somehow, we continued to live in powerlessness, toiling endlessly, and with little to show for our efforts. Our household economy was pummeled by our beliefs and assumptions.

## Becoming a Leader

At an early age I was called to be a leader in the Church. In the language I grew up with, I understood that I would one day be a pastor and lead people. I loved God and I devoured the Bible. Wisdom was like treasured gems waiting to be plucked from its pages. New Testament passages written to leaders and elders were important compass bearings for my growth. I learned stumbling blocks to avoid, and spiritual rewards to aim for. Serve with a willing heart. Care for the sheep. Be eager to serve. Do not be greedy for money. In fact, the "love of money" passages went hand in glove with my culture—we had just enough to get by, but I never had enough left over to fall in love with.

That's the way it is supposed to be, I assumed. I carried these beliefs with me through my youth into my early years of ministry.

As leaders, you and I find ourselves in interesting positions. We may have a title like Pastor, or CEO, or Manager, but if no one is following, we are simply on a walk, as the adage goes. Even as Christians we find ourselves being led by unfinished internal business rather than eternal truth. Expectations for ourselves—and those placed upon us by others—push us and prod us. And sometimes they bury us.

We are influencers, and in our design, we aspire to that. But in our desire to influence, we can bulldoze others with our illusion of power, knowledge, and "take charge" ability. (The one thing most schools do not teach us is to admit that we do not know the answer!) Or we shrink back and take the "slow approach," trying to win all the potential followers to best-friend status before leading the charge to a vision. And we end up going nowhere.

A lot of things have changed in my understanding of identity, roles, and the Kingdom of God.

## The Powerful Ekklesia

We are the Ekklesia, a powerful, legislative gathering of believers who make decisions that impact cities, regions, and nations. The Church is not a powerless and passive group separating itself from the world, waiting for liftoff. We are righteous warriors, not muted worshipers.

As Lisa and I took hold of this truth, our language and teaching were transformed. A few years ago, Lisa was teaching a class in the local jail that was having significant impact called, "Keys to Becoming a Powerful Person." A local Christian organization invited her to teach the course as part of an initiative to assist people out of chronic poverty. They asked her to remove the word "Powerful" from the course and eliminate language about Holy Spirit. Somehow those words communicated a message that those in leadership in some Christian organizations feared. Perhaps some worry it leads to pride. Or that raising up "powerful" people would release a rebellion of those who refuse to "submit" to leaders or pastors. Insecurity among professional ministers will result in the fear that followers might become more powerful than the leader. Powerless leaders reproduce powerless and ineffective followers. But confident and mature fathers and mothers launch powerful and productive children and followers.

The Ekklesia are the Called-Out Ones influencing their cities and the nations of the world, accomplishing Jesus' commission to "make disciples of all nations, baptizing them in the name of the Father and of the Son and of the Holy Spirit, and teaching them to obey everything I have commanded you."[5] This commission requires power and authority.

For this reason, God has given us the Holy Spirit and power, demonstrated through transformative gifts. Jesus has appointed fivefold ministries: apostles, prophets, evangelists, pastors, and teachers (Ephesians 4:11). These ministry gifts are created, not just for the local church, but for every avenue of influence. Businesspeople, government officials, school principals, fathers and mothers, actors, musicians, media moguls—God had intended that the fivefold ministry gifts be distributed among every aspect of human endeavor. Ministry was not simply for the "sacred" assembly of religion. It was for the Ekklesia to permeate every "mountain" of influence.

The message of the Seven Mountains redefines how we do church and missions in this century. These "mountains" of influence are religion, family, education, government, media, arts and entertainment, and business. We have seen that the gates of hell are located at the summits of these "mind molders of culture."[6] It is crucial to raise up leaders to introduce the culture of heaven to the tops of each of these mountains.

When I began in ministry, the focus of the church in that era was that the gospel of salvation be preached and delivered to every nation and people group of the earth. Salvation of men and women and children was paramount. The task was overwhelming in its scope. But discipling these converts and teaching them to obey? Herculean!

Then it dawned on us that Jesus commanded us to disciple *nations*.

It was like the camera pulling back from a close-up to reveal the whole picture. Transformation of nations was huge. That would require believers with authority in *every* nation. That would necessitate power and influence and credibility in every mountain. And it most certainly would mean learning the language spoken on each mountain and gaining access to the "currency" that speaks in every mountain—whether it is educational degrees, power and influence, or money, to name a few! God commissioned us to transform cities and nations. That requires power, boldness, economic clout, authority, and money to make practical changes that shift the culture.

In the church, I faced the Christian leader's dilemma: We were commissioned to a brilliant and massive vision of the transformation and discipleship of nations. But religion, under the enemy's influence, dug a rut that bypasses provision and empowerment for believers. Even as leaders in church or business, we often pulled back when we heard the words "power," "authority," or "prosperity."

In the Bible a chief steward was manager of a household of wealth. "The owner entrusted the management of affairs to the (steward): oversight of the property, receiving and paying bills, planning expenditures, apportioning food, and overseeing minors."[7] But suppose the owner would not give the steward access to the whole estate. What if the steward tried to set appropriate boundaries for the children, only to be informed that he had NO authority to teach them? Or suppose that the owner told him that if he wanted to pay the staff, he would have to work an additional part-time job, as pastors often do.

If you are a caretaker of an estate and you are expected to pay the owner's bills but are not given money to do so, you might want to find someone else to work for! If there is a legitimate repair needed, funds are released immediately to hire the contractor to fix it. How much more so with God? All power, wealth, and wisdom belong to Him. He is not on a fixed income, nor does He operate on a shoestring budget!

The overseer, in whatever mountain of influence, is God's steward according to Titus 1:7. If you are a city manager, like Erastus in Romans 16:23, or an elder managing church life like Titus, you are aware of the scope of responsibility and authority, and the expense required to get the job done. If God is the owner of the house, and He has an assignment for us to make disciples of all nations, then be assured He has the plans, the authority, and the resources to impart to His stewards to accomplish their mission.

## Pursue the Kingdom

Jesus reveals God's number one priority for humanity: Seek first His Kingdom. More than any other preoccupation for leaders, discovering and entering the Kingdom of God is to be our primary pursuit. The message Jesus spoke to Lisa, He speaks to people in ways that translate into every culture, every socio-economic level, and every situation: "So do not worry.... (Y)our heavenly Father knows that you need them. But *seek first His kingdom and His righteousness*, and all these things will be given to you as well" (Matthew 6:32-33, emphasis mine).

As Lisa and I continued our journey of trust with God, we encountered His faithfulness. We learned to recognize that we were not abandoned in our assignment. He cared about us! We were His kids, and He showed His willingness to come alongside us in our needs.

Just before He provided food and supplies to us, Lisa was shopping with our one-year-old. Easter was coming up, and our daughter had outgrown her one pair of shoes. In her beautiful Momma heart, Lisa was looking for nice little white shoes for our daughter to wear to church. She had to make a choice—eight dollars for shoes, or milk and diapers. She inquired of Father, seeking Him first, "Do I buy the shoes or the milk?" He very gently replied, "Put the shoes back. Go buy the milk." It broke her heart, but she put the shoes back.

The evening before Easter we had been invited to a family's home for dinner. Before the meal even started, our young friend suddenly turned and walked out of the room. In a moment, she walked back in with a beautiful pair of white leather shoes with little heart cut-outs, the perfect size for our daughter. "Could you use these?" she asked. Tears were all the affirmative response she needed!

A year later we were transferred to another ministry assignment while attending seminary. For some reason, there were major complications in the process of communication and decision making in this large corporate setting and I was not given a paycheck for my work for two months. I was confused, at first, and hurt. It was a Christian organization, after all. We had no money to buy groceries. "If he is so hungry, send him to Salvation Army" was the reply from the comptroller's office.

But Father wanted us to trust Him for our provision, not the church. Seek first the Kingdom. Look for His heart. We refocused our prayers, seeking God's heart, blessing those who were caught in a system that left us outside its rigid lines. And Father answered our cry for provision. Two of my bosses, godly men with hearts of gold, paid for my salary for those two months out of their own salaries. Father blessed us with provision from His body, the Church.

I can tell you story after story. God was demonstrating His love for us. He wanted us to learn to trust His heart, to experience His lavish provision for us both as His beloved children and as stewards in His house. His economy was accessible to us as we learned to seek Him first.

# 2

## Glory and the Economy of Heaven

If you have ever experienced desire, competition, and cost; if you have ever felt the sting of loss, the pangs of hunger, and the desperation of survival, then you have experienced the power of economics. Every longing fulfilled, every desire denied is an expression of economics.

Economics is simply the production, distribution, and consumption of goods and services. Every day, all day, our lives are intrinsically woven into these three aspects of economics. All of us produce. We produce food, clothing, intellectual property, or provide environments for raising a family or an atmosphere of hospitality for our friends. All of us are distributors as well. Distributors provide access to goods, services, and ideas. You might be a distributor of intellectual property or personal connections, a retailer, truck driver, or teacher. And all of us qualify as consumers. We need food and water. We receive love, purchase clothing, houses, and we have options of where to go for our education. Whatever your occupation or status in life, you produce goods or services, you distribute, and you consume.

All humanity is searching for fulfillment, purpose, and power. Even if it is simply to survive. This is what drives economics. In the early twentieth century, American psychologist Abraham Maslow developed a widely accepted concept he called the hierarchy of needs. He believed basic physical needs had to be met before people could realize their full potential. Maslow separated needs into five levels: 1. Biological and physiological needs (water, food, etc.); 2. Safety needs (shelter, protection, security); 3. Love and belonging needs (friendship, intimacy, trust, acceptance, family); 4. Esteem needs (dignity, achievement, mastery, independence, as well as desire for respect from others); and 5. Self-actualization needs (realizing personal potential, self-fulfillment, seeking personal growth and peak experiences.)[8]

If the primary purpose of most religions, including many expressions of Christianity, is centered upon meeting human needs as Maslow asserts, then the focus of their prayers, actions, sacrifices, and other forms of worship is driven by those demands. But human need and desperation do not drive Christian faith. Our existence and purpose are about a King and His Kingdom. The wisdom of Jesus turns the concept of Maslow's hierarchy upside down. Christians are not driven by need. They are led by the Spirit.

In 2003, during a hiatus from pastoral ministry, Lisa and I began a property management business for high-end homes. As a business we *distribute* a high-quality service for those willing to pay well for the excellence that we provide. Through this business we *produce* peace, safety, and well-being for our clients. This raises the personal value they have in their vacation home and the quality of time with their family and friends. To provide our services we must also *consume*—we have vehicles, fuel, cleaning supplies, laptops, equipment, and so on.

Whatever has value creates a demand. All our advertising has been by word of mouth. Every culture attaches value to certain resources and services. The higher the demand, the greater the cost. We have raised our rates several times over the years, and our clients have willingly paid because they recognize the level of service we provide and the value it has for them. This is true regardless of how primitive the culture or advanced the technology.

Several years ago, I watched the movie *The Gods Must Be Crazy*, a humorous depiction of the modern and primitive worlds colliding.[9] An empty soft drink bottle was dropped from an airplane into the world of a remote African tribe. With no previous exposure to outside civilization, they made the conclusion that the gods must have delivered this object to them. But what was it? Was it a tool for grinding food? Was it a toy for amusement, or a musical instrument? Did it have unknown powers to be revered? Whatever this object was, it became highly valued, even coveted.

The tribal members became consumers of the rare object, willing to pay a price to possess it, even if the cost was causing harm and division in the community. Ultimately it became a source of contention. This object became more trouble than it was worth! Perhaps it was a test from the gods. The hapless tribesman who discovered this "gift" resolved that it simply must be returned to the gods and dropped off the edge of the earth.

Likewise, we are consumers in a world with countless options if we are willing to pay the price. These "must have" items take competition to frenetic levels, whether it is food or the latest electronic gadget. We may be a modern society, but it hasn't stopped people from fighting over the latest Christmas fad in the community box store! Competition, desire, and covetousness are age-old experiences in new packaging.

Economy has become the most dominant expression of power and influence in our twenty-first-century world. Wars are waged with economics. Incentives and sanctions influence major decisions worldwide between nations. The Cold War against the former Soviet Union was fought with strategies of trade, sanctions, and relentless financial pressure. Wars with North Korea and Iran and China may be decided upon in the halls of government, but it is using the dominant influence of economics to bring pressure for change.

We feel the impact of economics daily. Corporations bombard us with advertisements. We may be oblivious to the influences of macro-economies on international markets, but we understand the language of financial hardship: unemployment, unpaid mortgages resulting in foreclosures, rising household debt, and phone calls during dinner demanding immediate payment—the weight can be crushing. Indebtedness is a contemporary slavery—socially acceptable, often self-imposed. Which of us has not felt stress, fear, shame, or helplessness under the driving whip of this world's economy?

As Christians and leaders, do we simply accept our economic condition as reality, set our jaws, and bulldog through it? Many have resigned themselves and their families to financial slavery, somehow convinced that it is God's means of teaching us patience and trust. For some it may seem the only hope for economic freedom resides in the end-time rapture of believers. "Beam me up, Lord, and let the sinners pay the bill!"

Where is our hope? We cannot escape the reality that every Christian participates in the world's economy. We may not be "of the world," but we are in it. We produce, distribute, and consume. But the foundation and reality of earthly economics go eternally deeper.

There is a fundamental reality that transcends bank accounts, stock markets, or political decisions. It is the reality Lisa discovered, higher than empty cupboards and an eight-dollar budget. That surpassing reality is the Kingdom of God.

Seek first and foremost the Kingdom. It is the reign and rule of God, the governing influence and impact of heaven on earth. This is the "King's domain," and dominion is the exercise of rule over that territory. Pastor and author Myles Munroe defines a kingdom as "the governing influence of a king over his territory, impacting it with his personal will, purpose, and intent, producing a culture, values, morals, and lifestyle that reflect the king's desires and nature for his citizens."[10] A kingdom is not a religion to be pursued. It is a dominion to be discovered.

Jesus declares our value, speaks of Father's commitment to meet our needs, and shifts our focus onto relationship with the Father.

"Your heavenly Father knows that you need them," Jesus says. Contrary to Maslow, Jesus does not start Christianity with the focus on man's need for survival, protection, security, or preservation. Our faith starts with God's declaration of His Kingdom, revelation of His nature, and recognition of our significance as His heirs. By seeking God's Kingdom, "all these things" will be given to us as well.

## Economic Foundations

Every economy on earth has its foundation upon something of great value such as gold, or a government's word that it is "good for it," (known as fiat). Society depends on the stability of an economy and its government. This stability provides the basis for currency. Currency is necessary. It is a common system that defines value for goods and services and a means to attain them. If a government fails to guard the basis for its currency by maintaining or even increasing its strength and value, the currency will become virtually worthless. I saw a copy of a check for a new car in Zimbabwe in the 1990s. Purchase price, over four quadrillion dollars. In 1922, one U.S. dollar could be purchased by the mark, the currency of postwar Germany (World War 1)—if you had 4.2 trillion of them! The mark was so worthless, they glued them together to make kites. Currency becomes valueless when the basis for it falls apart.

What is the "fiat" of God's economy? In the Kingdom of God, the basis for all recognized currency (allowed in any Kingdom exchange) is the generous heart of Father God. No one out-gives, out-spends, or surpasses the total worth of the Person of God. His ability to create is matched by His passion to give. The human heart, though given to desires for things of far less value, is never more enflamed than when it is sparked with the revelation of His passionate love toward us. Lavishly, unrestrained, He expresses His love toward us even while we are sinners, completely opposed to Him. Father God decisively demonstrated the intent of His heart and the extent of His love: "For God so loved the world that He gave His one and only Son..." (John 3:16); "If God is for us, who can be against us? He who did not spare his own Son, but gave him up for us all—how will he not also, along with him, graciously give us all things?" (Romans 8:31-32). What a stunning gift!

When we begin to grasp how much God values us, everything begins to change—our sense of identity, our decisions, our appetites, our relationships, the way we see the world and everything in it. Our worldview begins to transform. Our journey into the heart of the Father, the foundation of Kingdom economy, can begin when we encounter others who embrace us with love that is unconditional and sincere. When someone expresses kindness, drenched in the reality of God's love, doorways are opened before us into eternal, expansive rooms we never knew existed. Every threshold, once crossed, propels us into more dimensions of God's heart, compelling us to greater depths of discovery.

Perhaps it was from this place that Paul was revealing treasures to the church at Ephesus. I can see Paul walking into the Father's heart, opening door after door, overwhelmed at the gems, the treasures, the endless beauty in that eternal realm. Laughing at the sheer immensity and lavish gifts; weeping with gratitude and joy, he recognizes the cost of such love. Paul opens his spirit and soul and invites the people of God to join Him. "I pray that *out of his glorious riches* he may strengthen you with power through his Spirit in your inner being, so that Christ may dwell in your hearts through faith. And I pray that you, being rooted and established in love, may have power, together with all the saints, to grasp how wide and long and high and deep is the love of Christ, and to know this love that surpasses knowledge—that you may be filled to the measure of all the fullness of God. Now to him who is able to do immeasurably more than all we ask or imagine, according to his power that is at work within us, to him be glory in the church and in Christ Jesus throughout all generations, for ever and ever! Amen" (Ephesians 3:16-21, emphasis mine).

From that place of "glorious riches," Paul invited them (and us) to know this "love that surpasses knowledge." The apostle is taking us to the foundations of the Kingdom. Who of us can adequately grasp the reality of living life on this earth "filled to the measure of all the fullness of God"? Amid loss and failure, suffering and darkness, we dive into His expansive heart, and those powerful realities of His love become resident as treasures within our hearts. Those who encounter such unlimited beauty may not have words to express their experience. It is real, nonetheless.

Charles Finney, revivalist in America's Second Great Awakening, described his encounter with the heart of God: "(A)s I turned and was about to take a seat by the fire, I received a mighty baptism of the Holy Ghost. Without any expectation of it, without ever having the thought in my mind that there was any such thing for me, without any recollection that I had ever heard the thing mentioned by any person in the world, the Holy Spirit descended upon me in a manner that seemed to go through me, body and soul. I could feel the impression, like a wave of electricity, going through and through me. Indeed it seemed to come in waves and waves of liquid love; for I could not express it in any other way. It seemed like the very breath of God. I can recollect distinctly that it seemed to fan me, like immense wings. No words can express the wonderful love that was shed abroad in my heart. I wept aloud with joy and love" (Taylor, 2016).

John Wesley encountered the Moravians on a storm-lashed ship. Their peace and love launched Wesley on a Holy Spirit-led journey of discovery. With his heart "strangely warmed," hundreds of thousands of people in the British Isles and America came from miles around to watch this traveling evangelist and catch the fire of his passion for God. Wesley was once asked by a fellow minister how to attract an audience. He replied, "If the preacher will burn, others will come to see the fire."[11]

Such experiences of the fullness of the love of God result in explosive praise like Paul had at the conclusion of his prayer: "...to him be GLORY in the church and in Christ Jesus throughout ALL generations, for ever and ever! SO BE IT." As Thomas Dubay reflects, "We cannot drink deeply of divine reality without becoming irrepressible enthusiasts."[12]

## Father's Heart Revealed

This generous, expansive heart of God, the foundation for all that is of eternal value, is revealed perfectly in Jesus, the Son of God. With each healing, each sign and wonder, each deliverance from oppression, He exposed the foundations of the Father's heart of love. Jesus declared that He could only do what He saw His Father doing and speak what His Father taught Him (John 5:19; 8:28). Jesus is faithful to deliver Father's incredible gifts of love.

Did the heart of Father God impact the economy around Jesus? Turning water into wine may not fit the typical evangelical grid of "Love Languages," but it was obviously in the Father's heart to bless the celebration of the newlyweds. By responding to the bold request of his mother and participating in the lavish desire of the Father, Jesus uncorked heaven's treasure—at least one hundred twenty gallons of the best wine. That man received an economic windfall! John, by inspiration of Holy Spirit, remarks, "(Jesus) thus revealed his glory, and his disciples put their faith in him" (John 2:11b).

God's economy reveals His glory, and His glory impacts the economy.

An invalid of thirty-eight years was healed. A crowd of thousands were fed with five loaves of bread and two small fish. A blind man saw, and a dead man came back to life. With unconditional love, the Master and Teacher took the most graphic position imaginable to portray His heart to His friends, washing their feet even as the lowliest of servants would do. Jesus showed them the full extent of His love. A few hours later, His ultimate portrayal of His passion was made manifest before them upon the cross. "Greater love has no one than this, that he lay down his life for his friends" (John 15:13). Jesus engaged in stupendous acts of love, all revealing the heart of God. And every act of love ultimately impacted the economy.

## Father's House

As Jesus prepared to leave His friends, He said to them, "Do not let your hearts be troubled. Trust in God; trust also in me. In my Father's house are many rooms; if it were not so, I would have told you" (John 14:1-2). In typical North American circles, we would have a chat at this point about heaven and our mansion just over the hilltop. We would explain how someday Jesus would return and take those who trust in Him to join His Father in that place. But listen to how Jesus continues: "I am going there to prepare a place for you. And if I go and prepare a place for you, I will come back and take you to be with me that you also may be *where I am*. You know the way to the place where I am going" (John 14:2-4, emphasis mine).

Why did Jesus not say, "I will take you to be with me that you also may be where I soon will be"? Why did He use the present tense "where I am"? We know that Jesus had access to the Father, to His house and to His heart, while He was on earth. Could Jesus be saying that in the house of His Father, He was the door, and that Jesus was opening a way that would allow us access even while we are on earth? What if the house of the Father was more than a place of shelter? Could it include the Father's net worth?

The Son of God has prepared a place for us and given us access to the house of the Father, entrance to an infinite number of rooms with doorways, thresholds, waiting to be explored—here and now, not just someday when we die! Father intends that we access His house now, not just later.

In Romans 8, Paul talks about life in the Spirit of Christ. He says that we have received a "Spirit of adoption," or sonship. As sons and daughters of the Father, we are "heirs of God and co-heirs with Christ, if indeed we share in his sufferings in order that we may also share in his glory" (Romans 8:14-17). As heirs, we live our lives under God's favor. It is the intent of the Father that the sons of God be revealed to all of creation. Creation itself groans for that revelation (Romans 8:19-21).

The foundation of Kingdom economics is the heart of the Father. We access the Kingdom by seeking first the King. Through prayer and worship, with authority and confidence, we move and breathe, we ask and receive. This is the intention of the Father for each of us in His Kingdom.

Whoever heard of an heir without keys to the house? We operate with the keys *of* the Kingdom, not keys *to* the Kingdom (Matthew 16:19). We use the keys to release the power of the Kingdom, unlocking territories and systems shut up for generations. We use these keys to transform systems to conform with heaven's values, bringing entire nations into the light of God's culture. When we seek first His Kingdom and His righteousness, we gain access not only to places already prepared for *us*, but also to places once held by the enemy that we get to prepare for Him.

## The Father's Intention

Paul said, "All have sinned and fall short of the glory of God" (Romans 3:23). Our restoration to glory is the intention of the Father. The Giver of every good and perfect gift desires that we receive that which only He can give—glory. Kingdom economics is founded upon the reality and possibility of God's goodness and glory on earth as it is in heaven.

Glory speaks of the magnitude of God's personality. It is "heavy," tangibly weighty with authority. He is the most important and mysterious Person in all of time and space. He radiates life, filling the whole earth until it is full of His glory (Numbers 14; Isaiah 40:5; Habakkuk 2:14; Haggai 2:7). Radiant, unapproachable light surrounds Him. God's glory is the ultimate in honor, reputation, and dignity. It elicits the highest of praise. "Glory," says Bob Sorge, "imbues and sustains all of heaven. It is the air of heaven. The reality of God's glory in the heavenlies is more real than the seat you're sitting in right now. His glory is the ultimate reality. It is the tangible manifestation of the infinite beauty and splendor of His magnificent face."[13]

Glory is what happens when the reality of heaven invades the sphere of humanity. Explosions of beauty, restoration of life over death, health over sickness, mind-blowing and miraculous displays of the goodness of God move like yeast in every realm of life. When we pray, "Your kingdom come, your will be done on earth as it is in heaven," we are asking to breathe the atmosphere of heaven and walk in the reality of heaven and all its resources now, while on earth.

All glory is produced by God. Heaven distributes it to our hungry hearts. We partner with Him with the distribution to the groaning world that longs for the glory to transform their lives.

Glory, and our capacity to be restored to its fullness and covering, has been provided by Jesus, the Son of God. We may have fallen short of glory, but Jesus never did, and it was His intent to provide for His Father everything we could not—a perfect love, expressed perfectly and sacrificially. Restoration of glory is now our inheritance through Jesus Christ. As we respond with faith, we are opening ourselves to greater and greater discoveries of the goodness and glory of God.

## On Earth As It Is in Heaven

The Kingdom of God and its economy are not vague, undefined, theoretical concepts drifting on the edges of our minds. The gospels make clear that Jesus made teaching about the Kingdom an essential core, not a nebulous "secret." "Tell them the Kingdom of heaven is near," He commanded His disciples (Luke 10:11). The book of Acts is full of preaching the Kingdom of God and demonstrating the Kingdom in operation. While the Kingdom of God will be fully manifest when Jesus returns, it is not simply theoretical until then. It is here, now!

Understanding Kingdom economics requires participation in the Kingdom of God. The Kingdom is seen only by those who are "born again," and entered into by those who are born of "water and Spirit" (John 3:3, 5). Most parables in the gospels are explanations of the

Kingdom of God. They are pictures of righteousness and justice, often depictions of economics. These are stories that reveal the character of the King of this realm, and parables explaining what costs one could expect in transactions within His Kingdom. The Kingdom of God is all about the person of Jesus Christ, His life, death, and resurrection; His love and relationship with the Father and Holy Spirit; His reign over heaven and earth. The Kingdom is the reality of heaven's realm made known and released to the atmosphere of earth.

Jesus taught His followers to prioritize the pursuit of the Kingdom of God and His righteousness, pulling on the reality of heaven and the generosity of the Father's heart. When He taught His disciples how to pray, He was teaching the core principles of prayer, not simply what to pray. "Your kingdom come, your will be done on earth as it is in heaven" (Matthew 6:10).

Through prayer the people of the Kingdom of God invite the manifestations of the rule and reign of God among them. Heaven's reality and atmosphere are released practically in their families, their businesses, the marketplace, and in the nations of the earth. Transformation comes. Just as Lisa pulled heaven's reality into our cupboards through prayer, we pull that which is a heavenly reality into manifest experience on earth. The followers of Jesus preach and demonstrate the Kingdom of God, and transformation comes.

This is the foundation of Kingdom economics. Within the heart of God, we find the source of all that is of eternal value. And the brilliance of His glory is that He makes it available to you and me. Through us, glory is returned to Him. "For from him, and through him, and to him are all things" (Romans 11:36). Rise up, people of God. We have some exploring to do, some glory to steward, and some treasures to find!

# 3

## Stewards of the House of God

Foundations presuppose a structure.

On a beautiful lot high in the mountains, a foundation and concrete pad sat for two years. I drove past it often on my way to work. The view was amazing. It was located at the top of a ridge with views of forested mountains and stellar sunrises. I'm sure the owner rejoiced in owning the property and foundation, but it would be difficult to entertain guests around the nonexistent fireplace during our fierce winter storms. Certainly, the owner wants more than a foundation. He wants to finish the house.

Father wants to build a heavenly structure and make it fully manifest among us. He is not content with an unfinished construction zone. Father is intent on building His House, and He is committed to supply everything necessary to make it happen. God is looking for mature sons and daughters who will accept the responsibility and privilege to build and manage His House.

### The House of God

I have a business that manages and cares for private high-end homes in the Northern Rockies of Montana. I have seen some beautiful houses,

STEWARDS OF THE HOUSE OF GOD

room after room appointed with remarkable detail. My staff and I are responsible for the care of every detail of these homes, from pruning trees to painting walls, from mechanical checks to white glove cleaning. In each home there are scores of owner preferences, tens of thousands of details requiring constant vigilance.

It can take days preparing for the arrivals of homeowners. With attention to details, and a knowledge of the placement of every piece of furniture, every utensil, every hairbrush, the staff moves methodically and diligently through the house. Our pre-arrival inspections call attention to details missed—chipped paint on the wall, a spot on the wineglass, a misplaced throw pillow, a hair in a drawer. On the day of an owner's expected arrival, their estate has been repristinated, preferences honored, needs anticipated. The staff has worked hard to add value and an atmosphere of peace to the beauty of the owner's estate.

I cannot imagine the size of God's house. Brilliant, multidimensional treasures are stored in countless details of room after room in the universe-sized house within the heart of God.

The language of the New Testament opens a doorway to explore the expansive territory of the house of God. Paul teaches the church at Ephesus, "Consequently, you are no longer foreigners and aliens, but fellow citizens with God's people and members of God's *household, built* on the foundation of the apostles and prophets, with Christ Jesus himself as the chief cornerstone. In him the whole *building* is joined together and rises to become a holy temple in the Lord. And in him you too are being *built* together to become a *dwelling* in which God lives by his Spirit" (Ephesians 2:19-22, emphasis mine). Peter refers to each of us who are part of this Kingdom as "living stones" being built into a "spiritual *house*" (1 Peter 2:5, emphasis mine).

Every word italicized in these verses is some form of the word *oikos*.

*Oikos* is translated "house."[14] It is a dwelling place, a building or an estate where someone, in this case, God, resides. But *oikos* also includes the members of God's family, His generations past, present, and future.

So, the "oikos-house of Matthew" would include not only my house, but my wife, Lisa, my three daughters, and future generations. Those who are citizens of the Kingdom of God are part of the oikos, or house, of God.

Out of this root word come three words of special importance to Kingdom economics. The first word, **oikonomos**, is the "steward." This is the house manager or overseer given the privilege and responsibility of managing an estate of great wealth.[15]

**Oikonomia** is the *function* of the steward who oversees the management of a household or of household affairs, specifically, all that is part of the oversight and administration of the owner's estate. It might also include the role of accountant.[16]

**Oikoumenee**, the third word, is the totality and value of the entire estate. In the case of Father's house or estate, this includes the inhabited earth, the universe, all of heaven, and every dimension of creation known or unknown. *Oikoumenee* is the word often translated as "earth" or "world."[17]

These Greek New Testament words are the basis for our English word *economy*. The entire estate of God is His economy—His house, His offspring, His realm, His boundless resources.

I am constantly amazed at the sheer extent of this house of God and its economy. Consider the balance of the natural realm, the marvel of the microcosms and macrocosms of the universe. Every object is composed of atoms, the building blocks of all matter. In this microcosm, atoms are a complex balance of protons, electrons, and neutrons. Protons and electrons are electrically charged—the proton being the positive, the electron having a negative charge (while the neutron is neutral). The protons and electrons dwell in amazing balance to one another. Every atom in our realm is perfectly matched, several protons with the same number of neutrons. If it were not so intricately balanced, we would be exploding apart at the speed of light. If the charge of one proton differed from the corresponding charge of an electron by just one percent, the entire universe would be annihilated in a catastrophic explosion.

Put two magnets together. When the positive side gets close to the negative side of the other magnet, they quickly attract. But when you attempt to force two positives or two negatives together, they push apart. Understand the implications: In my physical body, there cannot be as much deviation as one part in a billion between any electron and any proton. If it were not so, I would explode into the last firework display the universe would ever see. A chain reaction would ensue destroying all we know. This physical universe, the *oikoumenee* of God, was created with stunning balance and precision. Such is the nature of His economy.

And then there is the macrocosm, the universe all around us. The Milky Way, our own galaxy, has between two and three billion stars. Multiply that by billions of galaxies known to be out there. Almost a billion light-years away from earth, IC 1101 is the single largest galaxy that has been found to date in the observable universe. This galaxy has a mass of about 100 trillion stars.[18]

What an extravagant estate God has created. And we have not even begun with the infinite, eternal dimensions of heaven.

Consider honeybees. Of all the geometric shapes these busy creatures could form to store honey, they chose the hexagon: six equal sides with six equal angles. The maximum amount of honey can be stored with the least expenditure of wax. Brilliant economic strategy! I suspect they did not have to hire the best mathematician among them to figure that out.

The pinnacle of all creation is man, fearfully and wonderfully made. Man was given dominion and authority by God over all creation (God's estate). Adam and Eve, legal guardians and caretakers of the estate, gave up their rightful place of stewardship of the *oikoumenee*. When they opened the door of God's estate to the enemy and ingested the fruit of the tree of the knowledge of good and evil, the first Adam signed the contract to manage the estate over to Satan. They removed themselves and all of creation from the "house of God."

Is the earth "the Lord's"? Yes. And all that is in it (Psalm 24:1). But the estate managers signed it over to another "manager" who steals, kills, and destroys. All of creation became subject to the destruction and death brought on by this squatter who gained legal rights to it but hates it with a passion. He wants to destroy it.

Satan, when he was tempting Jesus, declared brashly that the kingdoms of *earth* (literally, *oikoumenee*) were his to offer. (See Matthew 4:1-11; Mark 1:12,13; and Luke 4:1-13.) Jesus did not argue Satan's claim to management. The kingdoms of the earth really were Satan's to offer. "Bow down to me. Worship me, just this once. In secret. Nobody must know. Take this shortcut. You know that the kingdoms of the earth are what your Father really wants. Be a good Son. Give Him what He wants."

Jesus, the true Son of God, would not take a shortcut. Rather than worshiping Lucifer, Jesus walked through three more years of opposition, ridicule, oppressive accusation, and ultimately death in a most cruel way. He paid the price, redeeming humanity by His blood, restoring to His Father the legal right to the entire estate. Jesus, the second Adam, the brilliant son of the living God, won back the rights to the house of God—the same estate which the first Adam had lost.

And what an amazing estate. It encompassed more than the created realm of creatures, plants, and heavenly bodies. A new breed of humanity was being birthed. These born-again sons and daughters were His family, the Church, those redeemed through His Son Jesus. They were His temple, God's "favorite house."[19]

This is God's family, His house. Each family member is a living stone being built together. Each stone is a gem, eternally complex and valuable. Every people group, every nation of the earth contains brilliant treasures in its natural resources, and in its culture it carries seeds of redemptive purpose. These individuals and nations are the inheritance of the One who redeemed them with His blood. It is the privilege and responsibility of every son and daughter, the stewards of this estate, to partner with the Father in giving the Son His full inheritance.

## Orphan or Child of the Father?

The steward (*oikonomos*) is incredibly important in the plans of the Father. But prior to understanding what it means to be a steward, we must know what it means to be a son or a daughter.

For the past several years the Church has been returning to the necessary emphasis on the believers' identity as sons and daughters of God. The revelation of our identity as the children of God is imperative for us. If we do not see ourselves as son or daughter of the Father, we will have major problems with issues of identity. Consequently, we will misunderstand what it means to be a steward or a servant of the King of this kingdom.

Suppose I am the Dad. And I have *lots* of kids! Pretend that you are one of them, and you're at our house. You see some of the other children sitting on couches, and some racing to sit on the big brown rocking recliner (because it is my favorite!). But you choose to sit on the floor off to the side with a few of the other kids, incredulous that the others could be so casual and bold to sit wherever they wanted. Other kids run to a closet and pull out games. You watch red-faced as some of the girls have the gall to turn on the television (without asking!) and begin a video game tournament with a bunch of the others. Their play and laughter are infectious, prompting some of the floor-sitters to join them.

You are not so sure about this. *Don't they know that he is THE FATHER?* Confusion and uncertainty collide with propriety and sensibility. How can these kids who seem not much different than you act with such familiarity with the Father's things? And then the unthinkable... They open HIS refrigerator and start drinking HIS soda!

What do you think my face would be expressing if I were in the room? (Sitting in my favorite chair, of course.) If you really know me, you will know that I would be smiling. I love to smile. And I love it when the kids are having a great time. I am thrilled when they know that what is mine is theirs. We have a couch; use it. We have video games; invite the others to play! The fridge is there for the family; drink when you are thirsty. Eat if you are hungry.

My granddaughter recently said of our house, "We're going to my house for cocoa. I call it my house because it's warm and cozy and it's just like I live there." That articulates my heart exactly! And it expresses Father's heart as well.

Christians have been known to see themselves as orphans, living outside the privilege of family, existing as slaves, being in the house, but not of it. But you are a son or daughter of Father. You have been adopted, and you bear all the rights and privileges of His family.

## Identity Comes Through the Father

Our awareness of our identity makes all the difference to our participation in the economy of the Kingdom of God. If I see myself as an orphan who doesn't really belong, or a slave who performs out of duty rather than relationship, I severely limit my own ability to give and receive in the framework of Father's house (think, "economy").

My identity comes from Father. This became a major emphasis of Holy Spirit in my life as I walked with God in my own wilderness season of discovering my sonship. Let me explain.

My parents raised me in the environment of church. As a first born my identity became wrapped in my significance of what I did. As a child I was smart and received good grades. As a teen I was talented and received awards and honors. I grew up and pastored churches. There were accomplishments and accolades that fed my hunger for significance. And yet, I was neither satisfied nor fulfilled. Then my wilderness wanderings began.

Do you remember in Hosea 2 where the prophet says that God "allured" the bride into the desert to strip her of the old clothing, to wash her, and clothe her with beauty? That was my experience of the wilderness. Some of my "old clothing" were lies I believed about myself.

At the core was unbelief. I did not really know *His* identity. When I could be still and know that *He is God*, I could finally hear what He was saying about who I was (Psalm 46:10).

The desert really is a beautiful place. If you are there, or suspect you are going there, do not be afraid. You are in for some of the best vistas and experiences of your life.

He revealed my identity in the desert.

We all need an identity journey. I appreciate the enthusiasm of youth, particularly university-aged students, burning to "find themselves." I remember sitting in chapel when I was in college. Tony Campolo was speaking.[20]

He told of a student walking into his office, boldly declaring his intention to drop out of school for a year.

"Why would you do that?" Tony asked.

"I need time to travel, just get away. I need to find myself."

Tony thought a moment. "What if you get away from school, away from your friends and your professors, travel to God-knows-where, and discover at the end of it all that you are an onion?"

Exasperated and puzzled the kid plopped into the chair across the desk, waiting for the explanation.

"What if, while trying to find yourself, you peel off layer after layer of self to find the core, the essence, the purpose of 'you'? Assuming you *could* do that, what's to say that all the navel gazing doesn't find your purpose or your identity? What if after peeling off the layers, there was nothing left?"

Tony paused. The student thought a moment.

"What if you *were* all those layers? If peeling them off only brings tears to your eyes, you might conclude that, indeed, you are an onion!"

Identity is found not by pursuing *our* identity, but by pursuing God's identity. Let me illustrate in a couple of ways.

One of my daughters goes with my wife to buy a beautiful dress. She tries on a million dresses to find just the right one (the main reason I'm *not* there). When she finds the dress she really likes, she shows her mom. "You look beautiful!" Lisa gushes. Daughter smiles. Mom pays.

Then when my daughter gets home, Lisa encourages her, "Show Dad your new dress." Bolting to her room, she doesn't need any more prodding to try on the dress and parade before her father. Before long, she comes up the stairs, on her face a hint of a blush.

I see her. And I smile a really big smile. "You look beautiful!" I declare. She spins and twirls her dress around. "The dress makes your blue eyes just pop. Wow! You are gorgeous, my girl!" She giggles, holds her head a little higher, and steps a little further into her identity as "Beautiful One."

Why do my daughters need me to see them in their new dresses? Why not be content with what Mama said? She said exactly the same thing Dad did. Somehow, we are created with this need to hear the Father tell us, "You are beautiful."

I have come to see that my identity is established by my Father, through His confident declarations, His encouragement, His confidence. Mom can say, "You are wanted and accepted. You are precious. You are beautiful. You're going to be okay. You're smart. You're talented." But somehow, as the child I am only able to rest in those declarations as identity when it is recognized, confirmed, and established by my Father.

For years I listened to Mama church tell me, "You are (this)," and "You are (that)." "You are going to be (this) and do (that)." And it was right and good for me to hear the Mama say it to me over and over and remind me again and again who I was. But it was not until I heard the Father say, "Son, this is who you are," that my soul was able to rest, to be at peace. Then I could take real encouragement when Mama spoke. I could affirm, "Yep! I heard my Dad tell me that. Thanks for affirming that to me." And I could even say, "Hmmm. I don't know, Mama. My Dad never said that about me. In fact, he said it would be a good idea for me to take time to know him before I start getting busy doing that!"

Previously, I let the church tell me who I was. Some of it was accurate. Some of it was not. Confusion resulted. And all I needed to hear was the

Father say to me, "Son, you are..." Now it is a total adventure, even a game, for Father and me. I listen to specific encouragements from people in the Church, including prophetic ministry. There are a few chuckles and winks between Father and me, like hearing someone "read my mail" and Dad elbowing me and saying, "Didn't I tell you?"

If you want to know your identity, listen to Father.

## Identity Comes in Knowing God

To understand our own identity, we must know who God is. "Know Him" always precedes "know myself." Our desperation for significance, connection, certainty, or freedom can keep us in vicious pursuit of discovering ourselves. But Holy Spirit continues to lead us to focus our attention on God.

Jesus questioned His disciples, "Who do people say I am?" He paused after getting a few responses. "Who do *you* say that I am?" He asked. He took a sip of his latte, avoiding eye contact with the twelve guys, lest they feel undue pressure to answer the question and "get it right." He was thinking, *Man, Andrew's really getting the hang of this espresso thing! Perfect foam. I need to bring that up later.*

The twelve disciples had stopped breathing. Suddenly, pop quizzes seemed to be a thing of the past. This was a test. A BIG test. *Oh God, don't let him make me answer it out loud. How do I say, 'I don't know' without losing face?*

Then the big fisherman took a big breath and exhaled an even bigger one. God bless Simon. He had broad shoulders, able to take quite a ribbing when his mouth worked before his head was engaged—which seemed often!

"You're the Christ, the Son of the Living God," he blurted. There. He said it.

Jesus smiled into his foam.

He put his cup down. And with authority He spoke directly to the man, Simon, engaging his whole spirit, soul, and body in a revelation moment that resonated like thunder between them.

"You've been listening to my Father, Simon. You have discovered my identity and declared it openly to me and our brothers. Now, let me tell you who you are. You are Peter. You are not the irritating pebble in the shoe. You're a Rock, my friend. And on this confession which you have made, I am going to build my church."

Simon declared the divine truth of the identity of Jesus. When he did, the door was opened for Jesus to speak to Simon about who *he* really was.

If we really want to know who we are, perhaps we should spend more time declaring who HE is. Then be still. Listen for the voice of the Father. At some point in the quiet aftermath of your worship of God, you will hear Him say, "And this is who *you* are. You are my son." (Based loosely on Matthew 16:13-20.)

## The Son Is a Steward

Perhaps the church has misplaced important revelation about our identity and roles. The identity of the steward in the Kingdom of God, particularly as family members and heirs, is brilliantly conceived by the Father. The understanding that we are stewards of the House of God must be drawn into the slipstream of the truth of our identities as sons and daughters of the King. The momentum of the truth of our adoption with all its privileges and responsibilities can carry the reality of our role as stewards of God's estate to new places of revelation and understanding.

As people born into the new life in Christ, transformed in our agreement with Holy Spirit and the Word, we are now able to comprehend that we are perfectly created to build and care for the estate of God our Father. If His word says I am a "living stone," a "temple of the Holy Spirit," then it is true (1 Peter 2:5; 1 Corinthians 3:9, 16).

And I live my life accordingly. If I am a living stone, I must be shoulder-to-shoulder with other living stones, organically connected, building with them, and being built into a house in which God can take up residence. As a temple, my identity is one of purity, set apart for excellence and holiness. I am pure because I have thrust myself into the fire of His burning love.

The foundation of this new house has been laid. We are the living stones, being built into a magnificent dwelling for the Master of the house. Father is preparing this House as an inheritance for His Son.

# 4

## God's Extravagant Economy

In God's economy, calculators are virtually worthless. An army of accountants could never calculate His bottom line. Besides, who are we to audit the Almighty? And yet, He invites us to explore His vast estate, to discover what He values. He calls us to use the resources He makes available and to live daily on His provision. No matter how we look at it, God is wealthy. He has a massive house, an astronomical bottom line, and He calls us to administrate it. We need to diligently pursue answers to the question, "What does God's economy look like?"

Recall again the definition of economics. It is the production, distribution, and consumption of goods and services. Each of these elements is evidenced in the Kingdom of God, just as we see it in the economic systems of the earth.

### Kingdom Production

The Bible reveals the production potential of heaven in superlatives. "Now to Him who is able," Paul declares, "to do immeasurably more than all we ask or imagine, according to His power that is at work within us...." (Ephesians 3:20). This translation falls short of capturing the heart of Paul. God's production ability as understood by Paul requires an entirely new word in the Greek language. Only Paul is known to have ever used the word *hyperekperissou*.[21] *Perissou* means "superabundant in quantity and superior in quality; by implication, excessive." Paul adds to it the familiar word *hyper*, meaning "over, exceeding." He strings these superlatives together and says, in effect, "God is able (*dunamis*, like dynamite) to do exceeding (*hyper*), exceeding superabundantly (*hyperekperissou*), excessively beyond all we could ask or imagine." The sons and daughters must know that this power (*dunamis*, dynamite) works like His energy (*energoumeneen*) within us.[22] Imagine the unimaginable. Then stretch that…infinitely.

God can produce more.

Across the record of God's interaction with humanity, from creation to eternity, He produces in mind-blowing measure. "Is anything too hard for God?" The question is posed to Abram (Genesis 18:14). "Nothing is impossible with God," the angel said to Mary (Luke 1:37). Jesus presents the impossible possibility, "What is impossible with men is possible with God" (Luke 18:27). Multiplication of food, restoration of bodies eaten by leprosy, healings, resurrections, miraculous provision of finances… the list is endless. What can you imagine? His production capacity exceeds it.

The people of God must begin imagining again. If God can create *ex nihilo* (out of nothing), then isn't the economic potential within the Kingdom of God far greater than anything else humanity has ever seen?

My family and I have encountered God's production ability in numerous ways. In October of 1994, Lisa and I made a decision that, in hindsight, was crucial to the destiny God had for me and my family. We flew with our three young daughters to Fairbanks, Alaska, to hear Jack Deere speak at a conference. Although we had pastored ten years, we were unfamiliar with the things of the Holy Spirit. We were hungry, and we knew God was calling us into the pursuit.

I did not know how we were going to pay for the expense of flying my family of five, but we were confident that we were being obedient to God. We took the leap, flew to Fairbanks, and God began to rock our world with the truth of the power of His Spirit and Word. It was a time of demarcation for us, announcing a major shift and transformation in our lives and ministry.

Returning to Montana, we faced some real-life issues, among them the "how are we going to pay for that trip" dilemma. A couple of weeks later we received our bank statement and began balancing our account. There was $2,000 more in the account than there "should" have been. We went over and over and over the numbers. Somehow, we had more than enough to pay for our life-changing trip. How did it happen? I don't know. There was no record of a deposit being made! I just know that living month to month as we did, we did not have room for mistakes, especially ones that were exactly $2,000. Whether God created it out of nothing, or someone mysteriously deposited that amount in our account without it showing up in our deposits, we gave God thanks for His miraculous provision.

There have been many seasons in our journey where God has taught us to trust Him as our provider. Several years later during a particularly difficult part of our training, April 15th rolled around at a most inconvenient time. (Most American citizens recognize that date as the day our taxes are due each year.) Finances were extremely tight during that period of our lives. We were exactly $300 short of what we owed. At the time $300 was on the edge of what we could imagine. Lisa and I had plenty of experience in our lives with the faithfulness of God up to this point, but I was still learning to be at peace as I faced the final hour. (That is Matt-code for "I was freaked out and needing a solution, fast!")

At 9 p.m. on April 14th, a friend dropped by the church facility where I was worshiping and praying with a number of people. He handed me an unopened box; a night scope used for a hunting rifle. "I have been wrestling with God over this for months," he said. "I purchased it last September, and I knew it just wasn't the right thing to do. Today I was driving in town and Holy Spirit said to give it to you. Do you even hunt?"

We had a good laugh, since I was one of the few Montanans at that time who bought his meat in a grocery store.

The next morning, at his suggestion, I took the scope into the local sporting goods store, fearful they would not take it without a receipt seven months after it was purchased. (God's man of faith and power right here.) "Sure," the manager said. My heart skipped a beat as he took me to the cash register. He looked up the selling price: $299.99. I had to pick my jaw up off the floor. He turned to get the money and said, "Let's not worry about the change," and handed me $300. Exactly. God produces in ways that move beyond our economic grids.

## Kingdom Distribution

Every good or service that is produced requires a means of distribution, even those from heaven. With all the ability of Almighty God to create everything out of nothing, distribution should seem like a breeze. He speaks the Word at creation, Holy Spirit agrees, and the joining of Spirit and Word create the will of the Father and a universe is born. Throughout history, God found agents willing to agree with Him, and they became distributors of God's goodness. Prophets, godly men and women, and even ungodly kings, Balaam's donkey, and stone tablets—the list of potential means of distribution is vast.

The New Testament book of Hebrews recognizes Jesus is the Perfect Distributor. Through Him the Father "made the universe" (Hebrews 1:2). "The Son is the radiance of God's glory" the writer continues, "and the exact representation of His being, sustaining all things by His powerful word" (Hebrews 1:3). John the apostle calls Jesus "the Word" (John 1:1). The inherent nature of a word is itself a kind of distribution, a communication from one person to another. As "The Word," Jesus is Father's means of revealing Himself perfectly to humanity. "The Word became flesh and made His dwelling among us. We have seen His glory, the glory of the One and Only, who came from the Father, full of grace and truth" (John 1:14). "Anyone who has seen me has seen the Father," Jesus declared (John 14:9).

Perfect distribution is embodied in the person of Jesus Christ.

Jesus continues to distribute today through the Holy Spirit. He promised that He would send one known as "the Counselor," the "Spirit of truth" who would continue dispersing—forever (John 14:16-17). In Acts 2, we see the brilliant outpouring of the Spirit and power. This distribution was more than a breeze. It was "a sound like the blowing of a violent wind" from heaven that filled the whole house where they were sitting. Tongues of fire separated and rested on each of them. They were "filled with the Holy Spirit and began to speak in other tongues as the Spirit enabled them" (Acts 2:4).

In the coming of Holy Spirit and the formation of the Ekklesia, believers continue the distribution of the resources of God. In fact, the entire book of Acts is the stories of kingdom distribution unleashed. God wants His Kingdom on earth as it is in heaven, and *nothing* is impossible for Him. We are chosen to partner with Him. The Father is waiting for *us*...me and you. He wants sons and daughters to steward the Estate and faithfully administrate the distribution of heaven's resources. Are you available? The consumers are waiting, and they are everywhere.

## Kingdom Consumers

I like walking through my city. The downtown area, unlike many other Main Streets across America, is alive and vibrant. It's not that I am a shopper. I just love to walk and feel the pulse of my city. Sometimes I will walk into a shop and peruse for no other reason than to let Holy Spirit distribute to me and through me something of the grace and glory of heaven's atmosphere to that place of business.

Sometimes I leave with a burden. I feel the pain of an individual in the store or a lingering residue of anger. Loneliness. Or maybe fear. I will call a clerk by name at a grocery store while making a purchase and look him or her in the eyes (they are usually so surprised that someone would take the split second to read their name tag!). I often see the rejection reflected there, the search for significance, the pain and grief of loss.

Sickness and disease, injustice, oppression, unrighteousness, and death have emaciated humanity. The enemy has effectively stolen, killed, and destroyed. The fruits of his devastation steal headlines and fill conversations, reinforcing his power to distribute more of the same. Open your "radar" at work or in the mall. Perhaps you have felt what I feel—the pull, the void, the need of humanity.

Kingdom consumers are everywhere. Most of them just don't know what they are hungry for. People are crying out for peace, reconciliation in relationships, and stability in their place in the world. "When and how will I find fulfillment and significance, something to fill the emptiness and loneliness? How will I break free of this addiction? How can I endure this conflict? Will I ever be rid of this disease?" The consumers seek the fulfillment of their needs and desires, filling themselves with anything they can find and consume. Addiction, obesity, and overspending are evidence the longing cannot be fulfilled in lesser things.

All of us are consumers of God's resources. Paul spoke to the philosophers in Athens. "In Him we live and move and have our being," he said of God (Acts 17:28). Just as a branch detached from the tree withers and can never bear good fruit (John 15:4), I cannot even *live* apart from Him.

Remember Paul erupting in worship in Romans 11:36? "For from Him and through Him and to Him are all things. To Him be the glory forever! Amen." All of creation is a consumer, needing His resources to sustain and give purpose to life. All of creation is groaning, waiting in eager expectation, for the sons of God to be revealed (Romans 8:19-21). Why? Because we carry the fulness of the One who can free creation from frustration and the bondage of decay. Creation longs for the glorious revealing of the children of God. Whether man or beast, redeemed or not, animate or cold as stone, the smallest quark or the massive galaxies—all creation consumes the resources of heaven. As members of this glorious household and stewards of the vast resources of God, we need to understand the nature of our King and His Kingdom economy.

## The Nature of God

The nature of Kingdom economics is based on the nature of God. This is good news. It means that the economics of heaven is founded upon righteousness and justice. Integrity and honesty will never be lacking in heavenly transactions. You will never be cheated. The only fine print will be to your advantage, things like: "And we know that in all things God works for the good of those who love Him, who have been called according to His purpose" (Romans 8:28).

What is true about God? Generosity, joy, wisdom, and love are divine attributes. Even these barely begin the journey into the description of the Awesome One. Holy, sovereign, merciful, good, omnipotent, omniscient—with unhindered mental and spiritual capacity. We can spend all eternity listing His qualities and only scratch the surface of that which is true about God. What is true of Him is true of His Kingdom. Kingdom economy will never violate that which is true about God, for all heavenly goods and services produced and distributed will be stamped with His nature and character.

Therefore, we must spend time knowing Him. This is foundational to be effective distributors in Kingdom economics. No matter the good intentions of its architects, a temple is stable only when built on a solid foundation. Likewise, any economy is inadequate and will eventually fail if it is not founded on the nature of the King and His Kingdom. Transactions in the Kingdom of God will function brilliantly when we resonate with the clarion sounds of heaven, bringing the principles of our transactions on earth into alignment with the principles that flow out of His nature. Transactions without His righteous nature are simply a clanging, clashing disruption that eventually must be silenced.

Let's look at an example of how this works. Grumbling and complaining do not resonate with heaven's economy. Dan McCollam said, "Grumbling and complaining are the praise and worship of the enemy, and just as God dwells on the praises of His people, so the enemy dwells in the praises of his."[23] I seek to model this in my attitude and speech to the employees of our company. Grumbling and complaining are just not allowed. Instead, we focus on thanksgiving, words that edify and encourage, feedback that helps to teach and affirm rather than criticisms that tear down. We are developing an atmosphere in which God can dwell, even in homes that are not our own.

Rather than being anxious or fearful, we choose to work in peace. My role as a leader is crucial in assisting our people to choose the peace that is simply unreasonable—my translation of the "peace that transcends all understanding" (Philippians 4:7). When I treat each person with honor and respect, there is peace and joy among us, even when we have the pressure of impending deadlines. Attitudes of disrespect and resentment toward clients or fellow crew members are not permitted. We give blessing and honor toward everyone, rich or poor. We never allow curses, disrespect, or dishonor. This is the nature of my God. Therefore, it is the nature of our business to display His glory in practical ways.

What are the results? I am sure we have hardly begun to see the full extent, but here are some that I can share. Our crew has a genuine love, appreciation, and enjoyment of God, one another, and the work that we do. We have had clients comment they wish they could pack up our crew and take them home! They love their efficiency of work and the joy in which they serve. One client mentioned in passing that this was their favorite place to vacation, the most peaceful place they owned, a real refuge. Another fruit is that the business has prospered simply by word of mouth, beyond any business plan we could have manufactured. Kingdom economics has powerful impact because it operates according to the nature and principles of God.

There are many other principles of God revealed in the Bible to understand His Kingdom and its economy. For example, there is the principle of sowing and reaping. God could have instituted life from the beginning where growth was unnecessary. He could have provided every necessity and luxury without any output of energy from us. But He chose to set us within a natural and supernatural system of sowing and reaping. The seed you sow determines the fruit you reap. The measure you use determines fruitfulness. Even the attitude we have as we sow impacts the harvest. Jesus summarizes it by saying, "Give generously and generous gifts will be given back to you, shaken down to make room for more. Abundant gifts will pour out upon you with such an overflowing measure that it will run over the top! Your measurement of generosity becomes the measurement of your return" (Luke 6:38, TPT).

The principle of redemption is another powerful Kingdom truth in economics. Thank God that He redeems our ashes for beauty and our failures and shame for a double portion. As we offer Him our ashes, letting go of them and receiving our crown of beauty instead, the transaction of redemption is completed in the economy of heaven (Isaiah 61:3). Redemption is not limited to the realm of intangibles. Consider the story of Job losing family and flocks to disaster, yet God redeemed his considerable loss. Job 42:12 says, "The Lord blessed the latter part of Job's life more than the first." Peter wrote to a people who suffered greatly under the devouring and roaring of the enemy. But he made this promise in the Spirit of Christ: "And the God of all grace, who called you to His eternal glory in Christ, after you have suffered a little while, will Himself restore you and make you strong, firm and steadfast" (1 Peter 5:10). Redemption results in a strength that is important for stewarding wealth and prosperity toward increase.

Then there is the principle of offering the first fruits to the Lord. All we have comes from Him, and the tithe of our income is an expression of gratitude to Him. All the harvest belongs to the Lord of the harvest, and we honor Him with the first of the harvest we have received, whether wages or dividends (Exodus 23). As we receive bonuses or increases in our business, we give a first fruit offering to the Lord, thanking Him for the blessings—and we see more prosperity poured out upon us.

Many principles flow out of the truth of God's nature and His Kingdom. It is incumbent upon every believer in the Kingdom to know these principles and act upon them. Our effectiveness and productivity as stewards depend on it.

## A Sketch of Kingdom Economics

It is not possible for me to do justice to the massive scope of Kingdom economics. Imagine heaven with massive warehouses, storerooms overflowing with resources that exceed measurement. What is the desire of your heart? It may be intangible on earth. "Belonging" or "hope" cannot be packaged up and shipped to your door. But in heaven it is just as real or substantial as an emerald or ruby. They are stacked up on shelves ready for you to access. Other shelves hold blueprints for buildings yet to be built. New materials await distribution. An entire storeroom contains inventions yet to be discovered. New limbs and organs for physical healing are just as accessible. Wisdom for medical breakthroughs is available to the steward who asks. There are discoveries of systems that transform banking and international economies. New artistic expressions are available that will transform the arts and declare the glories of God. Resources are available for individuals and families, businesses, cities, and nations of the earth. The potential production of God's gracious provision by His sons and daughters is endless. It is waiting in the storerooms of heaven for us to distribute.

Breakthroughs in quantum physics are releasing a whole field of mind-blowing potentials, revealing the possibilities of multidimensional realities all around us. Christians should know it implicitly. The Kingdom of God is *within* you, Jesus said. It does not somehow come through careful observation of rules or signs (Luke 17:20-21). We do not have to go far away to retrieve these resources; they are as close to you as Christ is. We are seated with Christ in heavenly places, Paul says (Ephesians 2:6).

These warehouses, these massive storerooms, are accessible to you now. Eternal life, for example, is more than longevity in the afterlife. It refers to quality of life that is available now. What is the key that unlocks the door to that treasure? Believing in Jesus. It is faith that responds to the truth of who He is and what He says about me. I turn away from the mindsets that agree with death and agree that He chose and called me to live a new life in Him. My confession of faith is my wholehearted agreement that Jesus is the Son of the living God. Repentance and confession turn the key to the treasure that Jesus offered me, and I am reborn as a new creation in Christ.

Keys are available to us. "Ask and it will be given to you; seek and you will find; knock and the door will be opened to you. For everyone who asks receives; he who seeks finds; and to him who knocks, the door will be opened… If you, then, though you are evil, know how to give good gifts to your children, how much more will your Father in heaven give good gifts to those who ask Him!" (Matthew 7:7-8, 11).

Many years ago, our small Toyota was getting too small for our growing family. We were unable to afford a new car on our pastor's salary. So we applied the key of asking. With confidence and boldness we sought God for several months. One Sunday morning our church family called us to the front of the church and handed us keys to a van. Without a word from us, they felt the prompting of Holy Spirit and became partners in His provision.

To the rich young man, Jesus had a specific key that would open heaven's treasures to him: sell his possessions and give to the poor, then follow Jesus (Matthew 19:16-30). He went away sad, leaving the key behind. But Zacchaeus took up a similar key and unlocked the prison he had built for himself. He received salvation for him and his household and became a blessing of generosity to his city (Luke 19:1-10).

Paul learned the power of contentment in every situation in life on earth, whether in need or with plenty (Philippians 4:13). Contentment and thanksgiving activate a key that unlocks heavenly treasure rooms—confidence that God will meet all my needs according to *His* glorious riches in Christ Jesus (Philippians 4:19).

Faithfulness is a key. The one who has proven herself faithful with a little is given much (Luke 16:10-12). This is one of the most important keys to access for a steward. Your capacity to steward determines the amount of money or resource you are given. If you "bury" the treasure, you lose it! If you are faithful to take the risk with the resource and grow that treasure with hard work and wise stewardship, you are partnering with God as a royal steward. You will see increase! Kris Vallotton says, "(T)he invisible force of God continues to transfer wealth from the hands of the lazy, fearful people into the hands of the faithful, risk-taking stewards."[24] He continues by saying, "In the Kingdom, faithfulness is a sign of a wealthy soul and attracts money." The key is being faithful stewards of what we are given.

Sometimes experiences we have in life and our godly responses to them will open doors. Persevering in a trial of suffering or persecution gains us an authority and uncovers keys that can be used to serve others. I have seen couples who have been close to divorce submit themselves to covenant with one another and undergo transformation that has become a weapon of God against strife and division. The Spirit and the Word can forge our former chains into swords, weapons that dispatch the enemies and set others free.

Jesus said that we are to lay up for ourselves treasures in heaven. By storing up treasures in heaven rather than on earth, we can serve God as stewards of His resources rather than being a slave to mammon (Matthew 6:19-21). What does that look like? Most of us have assumed that "laying up treasures in heaven" means we will see the treasure released to us when we die and go to heaven. But what is the point of having treasures in heaven? Being bored is not on the program of eternity.

Heaven's vast treasures and storerooms *are accessible now.* What if "laying up treasures in heaven" means we are building the capacity of our heavenly warehouses and our ability to access its treasures for distribution?

When Jesus finished His conversation with the rich young ruler, He spoke to Peter and the disciples as the crowd gathered. "I tell you the truth...no one who has left home or wife or brothers or parents or children for the sake of the kingdom of God will fail to receive many times as much in *this age* and, in the *age to come*, eternal life" (Luke 18:29-30). This is a kingdom transaction which impacts both the future *and the present.*

There are treasures in heavenly warehouses that God intends to be distributed on earth in your lifetime. Imagine that we, the sons and daughters of God, the stewards of His entire estate, are pipelines for that distribution. Through us the King intends to send provision and resources necessary for serving others, and for making disciples of all nations. Our access protocol to these kingdom accounts, our unique PIN number if you will, is our personal relationship with Jesus Christ. Through us, as wise administrators of His glory, the nations of the earth are brought out from the kingdom of darkness into the Kingdom of light.

This is God's intention. He has given us everything we need for life and godliness through our knowledge of Christ (2 Peter 1:3). The production ability of heaven is endless. The consumers on earth are everywhere. The systems are in place for our instant access and rapid distribution to the metron we are called to for the transformation of the nations.

At the end of the age, there is a wedding. The gift Father intends to give His Son is a pure, spotless, blameless bride (Revelation 21). She is radiant in splendor, a fitting partner for the King of Glory. We are that Bride, called into partnership with Jesus to distribute His glory into all the earth. And Jesus in turn has a gift for Father—the nations of the earth restored to His original purpose and alive in glory.

# 5

# The Economy of Grace

*I awakened early. While I was making coffee, the gorilla showed up. I had been anxious to lose it the night before, but there it was again. Deep sigh. It slows me down, I know, but I can't seem to shake the burden and anxiety of responsibilities. Maybe it's a firstborn thing.*

*I made my way from the kitchen to the back deck. The air was cool, so I paced while I sipped my coffee. The task list for the day jumbled through my head; once again, more than I could possibly get done. Issues began to grind like sand in my brain, hard decisions, money issues on multiple levels. And conflicts. God knows I hate conflicts. If it could just be as easy as saying, "Stop it!"*

*My pace had quickened, my coffee had cooled off, and I didn't know if the gorilla was chasing me or if it was on my back. I suspect it had hopped on.*

*Have you ever had those dreams of being in the wrong place at the wrong time, totally unprepared? It all felt like a battleground where the enemy had all the weapons and strategies and high ground, and I suddenly showed up right in the middle of it with a toilet brush.*

*My rut-building exercise was interrupted by the Owner of the Estate. Frankly, I hadn't seen Him leaning against the railing of the deck. He motioned me over.*

*I mumbled some apology for not seeing Him and went and stood next to Him. He looked across the land and toward the city. His countenance was peaceful, even though I knew He could see every crisis that was brewing under the sun. Then He turned and looked at me.*

*"My grace is sufficient for you."*

*It sounds very different when He says it than the times I heard preachers say it in the past. I remember listening to a religious leader who influenced hundreds of thousands of believers give a moving and sorrow-filled story of personal loss. Heartfelt tears and well-crafted words exhorted us to keep going because, "'My grace is sufficient for you.' He's going to give you just enough to get you through. Not too little, because He's a big God. Not too much, because He has lessons to teach you. You will have just enough favor that you don't deserve to survive, to get by, to hang on until Jesus comes."*

*Well, when the Owner said it, it was very different. "My grace is sufficient for you." Each word released a wave of power. It was like hearing those individual words put together for the first time. Everything came alive in me. Somehow grace went from theoretical and intangible to the most powerful substance in the universe.*

*When He said "sufficient," it was like being hit with an explosion of light and color and water at the same time; like being caught up in a massive force of living water rushing toward a purposed destiny.*

*"My grace is sufficient for you."*

*In a moment He was gone. I knew I had everything I needed.*

*I should look up more often.*

---

Grace is a truth seldom understood and often trivialized. Sadly, even in churches, grace has become a nebulous concept in a Bible verse. Something that somehow gets handed to us in a gift-wrapped box by God that saves us. We know we have a responsibility to take this gift-wrapped box, tell other people how amazing it is, and hope they receive it. Meanwhile, we have never unwrapped it for ourselves to find out what it really is. We may have years in the Christian faith, yet still feel like we have an undiscovered box sitting on our desks under piles of books and papers.

God's truth-treasures have a way of surfacing.

For years, I wrestled with the traditional definition of grace I had been taught: "Grace is the unmerited favor of God." When I read Paul's greetings, "Grace to you," I could understand it. My mindset was that, as a Christian, I was still a "sinner saved by grace." God knew I did not deserve it. I read Paul's greeting as, "Matt, you sinner and scum of the earth, grace to you! Because Lord knows you need some unmerited favor!" Disgusting how the accusation and condemnation of the enemy can even twist scripture to reinforce his lies.

Then something completely unexpected exploded within me. In a season when God was confronting rebellion in my life, He also began revealing His goodness to me in stunning ways. The pain of my heart breaking under the weight of failure and sin was excruciating. But His beauty was breathtaking and restoring. And I began to understand grace in a totally new way.

Around that time, I listened to a series of teachings by James Ryle, "Grace, Grace, Grace," that gave me the language I was searching for.[25] Ryle cut to the core of the issues and gave me the tools I needed to live in grace. Let me share just the tip of the iceberg with you.

Jesus, the Son of God, lived without sin in His relationships with God, with man and the world. John writes in the beginning of the Gospel of John that Jesus was "full of grace and truth" (John 1:14). Does that mean that the Son of God was full of the unmerited, undeserved favor of His Father? No, He deserved every bit of favor that He received. So "grace" had to mean more than that. Here is the definition James Ryle gave that unwraps the treasure chest called Grace: "Grace is the empowering presence of God, enabling us to be who we are created to be and to do what He has called us to do."

Read that phrase aloud. Examine the New Testament references to grace (there are 123 of them). Let this revelation shift your understanding of these scriptures, renew your mind, and transform your life. Here are just a few scriptures:

"From the fullness of his *grace* (*His empowering presence, enabling us to be who we are created to be and to do what He has called us to do*) we have all received one blessing after another" (John 1:16, emphasis and insertion mine).

"Now Stephen, a man full of God's *grace* (*the empowering presence of God, enabling us to be who we are created to be and to do what He has called us to do*) and power, did great wonders and miraculous signs among the people" (Acts 6:8, emphasis and insertion mine).

"So Paul and Barnabas spent considerable time there, speaking boldly for the Lord, who confirmed the message of his *grace* by enabling them to do miraculous signs and wonders" (Acts 14:3, emphasis mine).

"For if, by the trespass of the one man, death reigned through that one man, how much more will those who receive God's abundant provision of *grace* and of the gift of righteousness reign in life through the one man, Jesus Christ" (Romans 5:17, emphasis mine).

"But by the *grace* of God I am what I am, and His *grace* to me was not without effect. No, I worked harder than all of them—yet not I, but the *grace* of God that was with me" (1 Corinthians 15:10, emphasis mine).

Now that makes sense to me. God's empowering presence *in me* has saved me through faith, not some nebulous nod of acceptance from an indifferent king. Grace is the presence of God Himself in us. When we receive "one blessing after another," it is from the fullness of God Almighty *Himself*. Grace is awesome!

But how does grace connect to economics and stewardship?

## The Steward's Grace

Every son and daughter of God has been given grace. Grace fills us, provides us with abundant provision to reign in life, and gives us the ability to walk in signs and wonders! The Apostle Peter had a revelation of the house of God, the Church. Didn't Jesus say that upon this rock He would build His church? In 1 Peter 2:5, the apostle says, "You also, like living stones, are being built into a *spiritual house* to be a holy priesthood, offering spiritual sacrifices acceptable to God through Jesus Christ." The "spiritual house" Peter sees is the *oikos*, the house of God.

Later in his letter Peter exhorts the believers who are this oikos, this spiritual house of God, to love each other deeply "because love covers over a multitude of sins. Offer hospitality to one another, without grumbling" (1 Peter 4:8-9). And then the apostle pulls out a treasure chest and sets it on the coffee table in front of us. Herein lie keys to the economy of God:

"Each one should use whatever gift he has received to serve others, faithfully administering God's grace in its various forms" (1 Peter 4:10).

These "living stones," which we have already come to see as stewards of the house of God, are given clear instruction and purpose within the Kingdom of God. Look at this verse again, but with the Greek transliterated alongside some of the key words.

"Each one should use whatever gift (*charisma*) he has received (*elaben*) to serve (*diakonountes*) one another as good stewards (*oikonomoi*) of the manifold (*poikilees*) grace (*charitos*) of God."

We have already begun unpacking the treasure chest by pulling out grace, the empowering presence of God. The root word for grace in the New Testament is *charis*.[26] Do you see it in the Eucharist? The Eucharist is the Lord's Supper or communion, literally "good grace." But it is there in the very same sentence in another word as well: *charisma*, or gift.

The gifts of God, and what we have learned are the gifts of the Holy Spirit, are essentially expressions of grace, the empowering presence of

God working in us and through us on earth. John Wimber, founder of the Vineyard movement, called spiritual gifts "gracelets."[27]

Pull them out of the treasure box. Receive them. Appreciate their beauty. They are intended to bring joy to you and those around you. These gifts, or gracelets, are powerful deposits of grace given by God. They are empowering gifts that enable us to be who we, specifically, are created to be, and to do what we, specifically, are called to do. These gifts are specific aspects of the goodness of God made manifest in His sons and daughters, each one uniquely revealing the glory of God on earth.

We receive (*elaben*) these gifts just as we would extend our open hands to receive a birthday present from a friend.[28] We don't seize it or remove it by force. The gift is offered to us, and we choose to respond to the offer, agreeing with it or not. It is not by our might, nor by our power, but by the Spirit of the Lord (Zechariah 4:6). We receive His grace and the gracelets which He gives so lavishly.

Peter reminds us later, in chapter 5, that "God opposes the proud, but gives grace to the humble" (verse 5). Humility is a prerequisite to receiving in God's economy. Put simply, humility is agreeing with God. It is arrogant to disagree with the Almighty. The son who wears the cloak of humility has the attitude of Christ which Paul spoke of in Philippians 2:1-11. Humility does nothing out of selfish ambition nor out of vain conceit. The humble man considers others better than himself, and looks not only to his own interests, but also to the interests of others.

Humility does not require self-deprecation. If Father calls me a saint, I agree I'm a saint, for it is humble to agree with God. If He says I am valuable in the kingdom, I agree that I am valuable. Too much of the church has been kept under a smothering cloak of false humility, which destroys the identity of the sons and daughters of the King and cripples their effectiveness. This religious spirit has stolen the birthright of many believers, convincing kings and queens that they are paupers unfit to lead, teach, or even think of doing miracles. As believers grovel under false humility, the grace and gifts of God available to them are never received nor activated in their lives. If we cannot receive His abundant grace, we cannot pass along His grace as distributors. The world is desperate to receive this amazing grace.

A person with a deceived, impoverished identity will not receive grace because of pride. A person whose identity comes from Father God celebrates their position of ridiculously good favor and receives grace because of their agreement with God. Which of these is a "good steward"?

As you reach for the next treasure, you experience the overwhelming love and compassion of the Father. As wonderful as it is to wear the "gracelets" and appreciate their beauty, this discovery releases purpose and the fullness of God's heart. Each believer should use whatever gracelet he or she has received to *serve one another (diakonountes).*[29]

This treasure is a vital key to release the economy of God. Gifts received freely from the nature of our creative God should be neither hidden from sight by insecure "slaves" nor used by spoiled sons to feed their own hunger for significance or control. In some parts of the church, the spiritual gifts are watered down and even discouraged lest the group be accused of fanaticism. But equally damaging is the church that uses the gifts to serve self rather than serving others. God-gifts may be given to us "without repentance" (Romans 11:29), but many of us need to repent of using these powerful gracelets for self-promotion, greed, or control of others.

Serve one another. As we have received these gifts freely, so we give freely, no strings attached. This is the koinonia, or the fellowship, in operation. Koinonia is actually an economic word meaning "sharers." Lavish expressions of love from sons who were formerly impoverished orphans reveal the glory of God. We become distributors of the gifts of God. When you touch His heart, it overflows.

Back to that beautiful box on the table before you. This gem will become a part of you. It will be like a living crown, or a badge within your heart. It speaks to your identity. Don't miss the power nor the privilege in this jewel.

How do we serve one another? How can we receive this empowerment from the Father and, with the full expression of His love, serve others? Peter says that we serve them as good, faithful administrators, economists, or stewards (oikonomoi) of God's grace.[30]

Okay, I am not trying to trick you. Very few of us get excited by the titles "administrator," "economist," or "steward." Sure, they are necessary and valuable to every business and ministry, but how could stewarding or administrating be a valuable treasure, even one attached to my identity?

Believers in Christ are "economists" *who determine how to best steward the empowering presence of God.* These stewards are mature sons and daughters of the King, each one given His power, through His grace, to do exceedingly outrageous acts of love and service. And the King gives each of us the wisdom to choose how to administrate or steward that grace. The King trusts you and gives you the freedom to distribute His resources just as a chief steward would with the vast estate of an extremely wealthy owner. Your capacity to bring transformation to the area of your assignment is stunning.

Peter puts no limits on his depiction of God's grace but adds an incredibly descriptive word: *poikilees*.[31] As you draw this last of the treasures out, I want you to see that this one is a party ready to explode! Translators use the somewhat stoic word "manifold," or the rather plain "various forms" for English translations. But *poikilees* is a brilliant word that refers to variety or diversity in a way that requires us to use our imagination.

Imagine a stunning rainbow splashed across the sky, and every part of it dances like millions of pieces of glitter. *Poikilees* is a party word! It is grace exploding into rainbow-colored glitter, each painted piece a glorious reflection of the beauty of God containing His unlimited power.

God intends that all this beautiful, dynamic, and powerful grace be poured into His sons and daughters and explode into manifestation on earth, just as it is in heaven. *This* is the grace that we have opportunity to steward.

## The Steward's Place

The church that I see today has an increasing, insatiable desire to receive grace from God and a growing boldness to operate with the gifts and callings of God. It is truly remarkable what happens when the people of God begin to outwardly live the life to which they are called. Nevertheless, I have seen an even greater number who have received grace but have grown disheartened, disillusioned, or discouraged. One of these reasons has to do with the steward's measure of rule.

Every believer has a "measure of rule" or "*metron*," a place in which he or she operates in authority.[32] Paul speaks of this measure in 2 Corinthians 10:13. "We … will not boast beyond proper limits, but will confine our boasting to the field God has assigned to us, a field that reaches even to you." Imagine a circle, your measure of rule, your "field" assigned to you by God. You probably never received an email or an office memo from heaven detailing to you where the boundaries of your field lie. Thus, we find many Christians and pre-Christians wandering about murmuring that "we just don't know where we fit." Do not be harsh with those who don't know. Their grumbling will not help them find their measure of rule, but neither will our accusation. Extend to them the grace you have received.

If you are casting about to find your place assigned by God, take some steps to enter into His grace. First, worship God and give Him thanks. Second, listen for His declaration of who you are. Third, listen to Holy Spirit. What is He revealing to you? Finally, step into it. As you do, you will find yourself discovering the boundaries of your metron.

You have permission and freedom to explore, to find out where you belong. Here is a crucial test: Where the Spirit of the Lord is, there is freedom (2 Corinthians 3:17). Your spirit and soul must be in a place where it has permission to listen, free to decide and free to act. Our first response typically is to blame leadership in our churches for our feeling that we don't fit, that we are held captive by "their lack of vision," or that there is no space for "my ministry." Do not cast responsibility for your freedom on someone else. Freedom is a choice. Be free.

Within your measure of rule, God gives grace. When you are doing what you are called to do, being who God created you to be, you know His empowering presence. You feel energized, alive, and fulfilled. But when you are pretending to be someone else or doing something outside the circle of your measure, you are operating in your own strength, without grace. The great thing with God is that, even though you have stepped outside the measure He has assigned you, you have stepped into a buffer zone called "Mercy."

Thank God for mercy. It is the safety net of His unmerited favor and kindness. It is His unending smile that encourages us, picks us up, wipes the blood off our skinned knee, and sends us back into the game. I love His mercy. But the realm of mercy is not the place that I am created to live in. It is the place that reminds me that I need to make a change. I need to get back to the place where I can feel His energy working powerfully in me, where grace flows once again. When you step outside the boundaries of your measure of rule, the grace stops flowing. Do the gifts stop operating? No. But there is significant reduction in Kingdom impact on others when you step outside of your measure.

The great kindness of God's design is this: When you no longer feel the empowering of God for your days, your work, your family, or your ministry, the buffer zone around your circle is created by God to encourage you to get back into your measure. No passion? No energy? No fulfillment? The place of mercy gives you a safety zone in which to be still and get to know God's heart and mind. When you find that place of His kindness, take steps to find the place where you are energized once again.

In the early years of our business working for a client, we made a terrible mistake. We were filling a sink in the kitchen. Something distracted our attention in another room and it wasn't until several minutes later, to our horror, that we discovered water running across the floor and into the ceiling of the room below. We really messed up. That was a very difficult phone call to make!

Our client was incredibly merciful. He was so kind.

"Well, I bet you don't do that again. What are you going to do about it?"

He gave us the opportunity to clean up our mess and show him he could trust us. Being a steward was not about getting it perfect but putting things right and growing through it. His mercy built our confidence to fix our mistake, and our rapid response built his trust. It was a costly repair but as we stewarded our mistake with integrity to restore value to his property, the expense was rewarded. It was right after that that he started referring us to his friends.

Is there an area of disobedience or sin? If Holy Spirit convicts you of any sin, do not beat yourself up about it. Mercy will remind you. Repent and get back into that circle of grace. If there is no sin, it may be that your metron is simply shifting to another measure.

Our measure of rule can change. In fact, for some it can change more frequently than for others. Perhaps you felt God's grace in a particular ministry for several years. But it seemed like the "juice" just left you. You were not motivated to engage in that expression of ministry like you knew before, and the fruitfulness no longer followed you.

I left full-time professional ministry as a pastor in 2002. I believed it was in obedience to God. Working odd jobs was difficult. My internal need for significance was definitely not being met. But I began to find my new measure of rule. The most difficult part was accepting that I was okay. I was not backslidden or disobedient. I was not a failure. There were some who felt obligated to castigate me and relegate me to the category of "isn't it a shame what happened to him." But I was in a great season of being stripped of old mindsets and learning what my Father said of my identity and destiny.

Sometimes God can move your circle to equip you for a larger metron. In Montana there are a great number of farms and ranches.

Dad and Mom assign each of their children a few chores. All the kids are growing, maturing, and learning new skills, increasing in their knowledge. As they do, rancher Dad has no problem changing the chores for the sons and daughters. The sixteen-year-old is plenty strong enough now to dig postholes and string fence. The seven-year-old, on the other hand, is learning the discipline of mucking out the stalls. Chores will change. God moves our circles. This is important in order for a son to understand all aspects of his father's business. It is a process of becoming mature and ready to run the ranch.

Explore. Find where the grace flows again as you put your skills, resources, and gifts to work serving others. And remain sensitive to the seasons of discipline, rest, warfare, and work. Enjoy God in the process of the expansions of your measure of rule.

Pull that treasure box out often. Appreciate the gems that the Apostle placed in there by Holy Spirit's inspiration. He exhorts me and you to faithfully administrate the brilliant expressions of God's grace which we have received to serve one another. He goes on to say, "If anyone speaks, he should do it as one speaking the very words of God. If anyone serves, he should do it with the strength God provides, so that in all things God may be praised through Jesus Christ. To him be the glory and the power for ever and ever. Amen" (1 Peter 4:11). Each of us is given resources produced in heaven. As we steward these resources, we do so intentionally, with the fear of the Lord, empowered by the Spirit of the Lord and with His joy.

Now that is a picture: A wise and worshiping administrator, hopelessly in love with God and laughing hilariously while giving away as much as he possibly can.

I think I can enjoy this Kingdom's economy.

# 6

## The Art of Distribution

I love to play jazz. It is amazing to watch people drawn into sounds and rhythms. Different music and rhythms evoke a variety of movements and emotion. A group of my musician friends and I played several times at a senior living residence. What a joy to watch their faces light up as we played songs popular in the 1930s and 1940s! Some of them would get to their feet and dance with renewed vitality to the songs they knew and loved in their youth. I have seen a few sitting at their tables with tears in their eyes, silent tributes to memories strumming the heart strings of their souls. All we did was play old jazz music.

But think about what was required of us as musicians. We had to do more than make sound with our instruments. Each of us knows our instruments well. Each of us learned music over years of practicing scales and rhythms and chords. We played from the foundations of excellent musicianship. But reading and playing music are not enough. Our ears are trained to listen to one another, to feel the movement of the song and provide space for one another to release spontaneous expressions of melody and harmony. All the intricacies, all the pieces, work together to make the song unique. It takes a song into places it has never been and takes the audience into a new experience of a familiar sound.

The complexity and beauty of heaven's economy is akin to an art form. Distribution of heaven's resources is intended to be a moving experience.

Economic systems require distribution. From raw materials to finished products, delivery requires massive investment of resources. Consider the costs of developing transportation systems, not only trucks, trains, and planes, but the highways, rail systems, and airports. Underground pipes move water and gas to every building. Wires transfer electricity. We are inherently dependent upon distribution at every level of our lives. Oxygen, water, heat, food, even thoughts and the body's sensations require methods and pathways for distribution.

In the Kingdom of God, stewards are conduits of grace. We are distribution pipes for heavenly resources, dispensing the gifts of God lavishly upon the earth. We have the keys of the house of God and can release provision and resources. As administrators, it is not enough just knowing *what* the house contains. Our job is to know and to distribute those resources faithfully and wisely. Let us look briefly at some of the basics of distribution as it relates to the steward, and then relate it to concrete examples of stewarding in life.

Another way of looking at distributing heaven's treasures is the imagery of a pipeline. I'll call this the "Oikonomos Pipeline." It has three essential elements: connection to heaven; connection to earth; and creative connections.

## 1. Connection to Heaven

A pipeline must be securely connected to its source. A garden hose must be connected into the spigot or we won't get water to the garden fifty feet away.

Nicodemus, a member of the Jewish ruling council, hungered for the truth he experienced through the miraculous signs in the ministry of Jesus. Jesus explained to him the source of this power was in the Kingdom of God and connecting to that source requires believing in (literally, *into*) the Son of God (John 3:16). Jesus provides access to the Father and His

Kingdom. We actively connect to the Father by continuing in our faith, "established and firm, not moved from the hope held out in the gospel" (Colossians 1:23).

If the heart of the Father is the source (the endless water supply), then Jesus is the access point, the spigot. By faith we connect our hose to the spigot for the flow of living water.

We are all "fellow citizens with God's people and members of God's household," as Paul says (Ephesians 2:19). As citizens of the kingdom of God we remain connected to the King and His kingdom. At this very moment, you and I are seated with God "in the heavenly realms in Christ Jesus" (Ephesians 2:6). We have access at any time to the throne of grace from which flows the River of Life (Hebrews 4:16; Revelation 22:1).

This is the Steward's Imperative: Set your heart and mind on things above (Colossians 3:1-2). If Christ is in me, and my life is hidden with Christ in God, then I can think the thoughts of Christ and feel the heart of the Father. In fact, "we have the mind of Christ" (1 Corinthians 2:16).

The Oikonomos Pipeline must remain connected to the source of all heaven's goods and services so distribution can be made manifest on earth through us. Jesus clearly stated that even He, as both man and God, did only what He saw His Father doing, and His words were not His own, but "the Father, living in Me, who is doing His work" (John 14:10).

## Connecting to Heaven Includes Knowing God's Preferences.

To effectively administrate or steward the economy of God's kingdom, we need to know what God wants. "Find out what pleases the Lord," Paul exhorts us (Ephesians 5:8-10).

This is massively important. The King's preferences always take precedence over the servant's desires. In my business as a household manager, the owner's tastes and preferences are more important than mine. I may have opinions about the color of the walls, the locations of the sofas, and the style of the painting in the study, but I do not sell the couch and painting and start a remodel project. I do not rearrange the furniture. I must know the owner's preferences and actively contend for that which pleases them. If they were to ask me to build something, I would build it according to their plan and not my own.

But knowing a client goes beyond knowing how they like their pillows placed and how they like their toilet paper folded! I must understand their heart's desires. When they come to their vacation house they are looking for rest, peace, fun, and connection. What separates a steward from a common servant is knowing more than to-do lists but anticipating their needs and desires.

A client was coming to their new estate, excited to enjoy a vacation with their young children. We finished detailed preparations the day before arrival. When I went to bed that night, I asked Holy Spirit to show me anything I needed to know for arrival. I had a dream that I was walking through the house, and into the baby's room. On the windowsill was a large nail—just above the crib. The next day I found the nail, just where Holy Spirit showed me it would be. He knows a parent's desire for a child's safety. So He allowed me to help provide for that.

A marriage relationship portrays the importance of knowing one another. When Lisa and I were newlyweds, it was difficult anticipating each other's needs and preferences. One evening, three months into our marriage, I walked through the front door and was greeted by a familiar but unwelcome smell. Dinner was in the oven—a recipe enthusiastically endorsed by my mother as "one of Matt's favorites." It consisted of white bread, white gravy, eggs, salt, and pepper, mashed together into a casserole. Lisa said my face grew pale. I sat down at the table with my tentative bride. We offered tidbits about the day and tried to spoon the concoction past our taste buds. No offense to anyone who enjoys egg casserole, but it was hard to smile with egg slithering down my throat.

After an awkward moment of silence, I worked up the courage.

"Ummmm." It was not a bold start. "Would it be okay if we don't have that again?" She was relieved! She suffered through it, anticipating this was a dish I *"really* liked!" The years together have been awesome for learning one another's tastes and preferences. It takes time together, talking, observing, and noticing details that few others know for us to participate in that kind of relationship.

As stewards, we can anticipate the desires of the King by immersing ourselves in revelation, understanding and knowledge packed within the inspired words of the Bible. By studying scripture, we discover God's intentions and plans, His thoughts and preferences, and discover what He really values. Jesus explained the kingdom of heaven in numerous parables (as recorded in Matthew chapter 13). "Therefore every teacher of the law who has been instructed about the kingdom of heaven is like the owner of a house who brings out of his storeroom new treasures as well as old" (Matthew 13:52). A steward of the master's estate would do the same. The Old Testament treasures are affirmed by Jesus. But the New Testament teachings of the kingdom of heaven are treasures as well. Today's stewards who know Jesus' instruction of the kingdom of heaven will understand His heart and serve Him well.

This flow of power and life is constant. "Be filled and keep on being filled with the Holy Spirit" (Ephesians 5:18b, *translation mine*). What a stupendous, fabulous privilege we have as the sons and daughters of God. We are not orphans, left alone to struggle against our own world systems, or wrestling with forces of darkness. The Creator embraces us, loves us to life, and breathes His Spirit into us. We see like we have never seen before and hear like we have never heard. How easy it is to give thanks to God our Father for everything in the name of Lord Jesus Christ. The Spirit of the living God lives and moves and brings forth powerful streams of living water, *within us.* We flourish when we walk in the fullness of the Holy Spirit.

Holy Spirit takes what belongs to Father and Son, and imparts to us, and releases it through us (see John 14:26; 15:26; 16:5-15). He is everything we love about heavenly distribution. His ever-flowing generosity delivers exactly what needs to be allocated at just the right time. As the Ekklesia we have the ability to tap into that flow and distribution God's resources as needed.

## Connecting to Heaven requires both The Spirit and the Word

In creation, "the Spirit of God was hovering over the waters" (Genesis 1:2). Chaos was churning, but the Spirit brooded over the chaos. "And God said, 'Let there be …' and there was …" (1:3, etc.). The word went out, the Spirit joined in agreement with the word spoken, and creation happened. Order was established where chaos had reigned. And man, crowned with the glory of God, exercised dominion over creation. Distribution of heaven's resources and the glory of God require both Spirit and the Word together.

Over and over the pattern is repeated in the Old and New Testaments. Obedience to the word *plus* the anointing and grace given by the Spirit, *resulted in* the glory of God manifest on earth. Simply put, Word + Spirit = Divine Order and Glory.

For example, the *word* came to Moses to build a tabernacle according to the pattern God gave him (Exodus 35:11). Craftsmen with the *Spirit* of God exercised their leadership and skill, establishing the *order* of the tabernacle exactly as God had revealed to Moses (Exodus 35:30-36:1.) The cloud covered the Tent of Meeting, and the *glory* of the Lord filled the tabernacle (Exodus 40:35).

The temple in Solomon's time was built with the same pattern. Faithful men and women responded obediently to the *word* and the *Spirit*, resulting in God's *order* (2 Chronicles 1-6.) "Then the temple of the Lord was filled with a cloud, and the priests could not perform their service because of the cloud, for the *glory* of the Lord filled the temple of God" (2 Chronicles 5:13-14.)

One hundred and twenty disciples of the resurrected Jesus gathered in obedience to his *word* to wait for a while in Jerusalem. Their obedient response to the word was met with the coming of *Holy Spirit*, establishing a whole *new order* of humanity in birthing the Church. *Glory* was manifest brilliantly (Acts 1-2).

What was true then is true today. Stewards respond with agreement and obedience to God's word, empowered by Holy Spirit. Sons and daughters filled with the Spirit hear the word from heaven and chaos is overthrown. God's Kingdom order is established on earth as it is in heaven, and the glory of God is made manifest in greater measure.

## Connection to Heaven Involves Knowing the Resources

As faithful stewards allocating heavenly resources, we need to know what those goods and services are. What are the tools necessary for cultivating faith? What are the weapons for warfare? What are the treasures of heaven available for distribution?

On a few occasions, I have walked into hardware stores in search of specific products and been met with completely helpless staff. They were powerless to help me find what I needed because they were unfamiliar with the contents of the store and where the products were located. I adopted an attitude: Save time. Don't ask.

Stewards are powerful people. They are disciples, constantly learning and intimately connected to the One who gives good gifts. The world is looking for men and women who have real answers to real problems, not apologetic, powerless people who are trying to look busy 'til Jesus comes. Do we know how to access heaven's creative solutions? If there is a problem in a relationship, God has keys to unlock the issue and bring godly resolution. Businesses in trouble need the wisdom of God's people to untangle the mess. Environmental chaos requires stewards who are attentive to God's strategies.

What do we do? Get God's heart and receive the word of the Lord. Speak the word, in agreement with the Holy Spirit. Our faithful obedience to the word on earth connects the Oikonomos Pipeline to heaven.

The world needs those who are connected to heaven. "For from Him and through Him and to Him are all things."

## 2. Connected to Earth

It may seem like a given that stewards are connected to earth, but frankly some Christians have disconnected themselves from the world around them. There is a strong belief in the Christian church that values intangible over tangible, metaphysical over physical. Spirit is good, body is bad; so, we elevate the ethereal and mistreat the physical. Even our eschatology, our theologies of the end times, can lead us into the temptation of being irresponsible and unjust in our treatment of our physical bodies, practical financial decisions, or environmental decisions with long-term implications. "If we are only going to be here a short while," we argue without words, "and it all goes up in smoke anyway, why worry about it?"

We must connect and engage all around us in this earthly realm. God created and loves these people and this creation. Not just their spirits; but their whole person! Not just the individuals, but entire nations. Justice, for example, is not simply a theoretical concept held by God. It is highly valued by God, a foundation to his throne (Psalm 97:2), essential to godly authority. We engage earth's relationships, businesses, international affairs, etc., with the justice of God that overwhelms injustice through its massive strength and perseverance.

In the past generation it has been in vogue for churches to write their vision statements and values. A few live out their values. A vast majority simply clothe themselves with the value statements, parading it on Sunday, but hanging it up for the rest of the week. Intellectual assent and majority consensus do not make it a value. Living it does.

THE ART OF DISTRIBUTION

As stewards of the house of God we value what the Master values. Our lives reflect the importance God gives to something. If He says to honor, we honor practically with our words and our actions. If He says, "Don't covet," then we do more than just quote the Ten Commandments ritualistically. We learn to be content, and we refuse to cave in to unrighteous desire.

A fundamental responsibility of the Steward in Kingdom economics is to *create value*. In economics, someone creates value for goods or services. Generate a demand for something, and people will pay more. Black pearls were considered flawed, a fraction of the value of white pearls, until someone placed them in a luxury store window in New York City with a price tag well above that of the white pearls. Human behavior seems to be influenced easily: Make something difficult to attain, create high value, and people will covet it. The suppliers could not get black pearls to the jewelers fast enough.[33] Find the value in the ordinary and make it extraordinary. Take what is considered worthless and make it priceless.

We are the salt of the earth, creating hunger and thirst for God and His kingdom wherever we go (Matthew 5:13). We bear good fruit that creates value all around us. Have you ever been in the presence of the Lord, experiencing his peace and life, and then gone out to run errands? People notice there is something that draws them to you, but they cannot quite put their finger on what it is. We create value through the atmosphere we produce as we abide in Christ.

The way Christian stewards spend resources impacts earthly value. If we use our resources (time, talents, money, etc.) in obedience to God, to pursue Him and His Kingdom, it activates an anointing that attracts others to God and his Kingdom. If we use the resources to promote self, it carries power to attract people to ourselves—or possibly repel them. If we use these resources to engage in sin, it attracts others to engage in that same sin. Stewards carry authority that opens significant pathways, establishing value on earth, whether positive or negative.

We can establish value on earth as stewards of God's economy simply through our patronage in different businesses. We bless that establishment with God's presence just by being there. My family and I see this often.

Lisa and I walked into an empty restaurant late one night to eat some pie and talk. It was a date night. We noticed the restaurant was empty and it appeared they had been preparing to lock up a couple of hours early. The staff served us our pie and kept vacuuming. Within ten minutes of arriving I noticed the vacuum cleaner had been turned off. Groups of people were showing up; more than twenty-five people had decided they wanted to stop *there* to eat. That might be coincidence if it happened just once or twice. But it has happened to us time after time. My daughters smile when we walk up to an empty counter in a sparse restaurant, order, and walk to our seats through crowds of people.

To some that might sound farfetched. But stewards of the King carry grace, the presence of God, which is a fragrance drawing other people to them. Our simple choice of where to eat may compel others to follow. I am convinced that pathways of blessing and favor are opened through our simple, seemingly insignificant choices. The concept is exciting and sobering, for creating value is a significant responsibility for the Body of Christ. We establish value through our generosity, tipping our waitress, giving gifts anonymously. Speaking kindly and with honor is amazing and powerful in our culture.

We were on a relatively long waiting list for a restaurant in a popular amusement park. I requested a table outside. The family and I waited awhile, a bit tired but enjoying each other. Our hostess, a kind woman but obviously weary, called our name.

"We have a table available indoors," she offered.

"No problem," I smiled.

She paused, knowing we had requested a table outdoors, and with a "Just a moment," disappeared back into the restaurant. A minute later she returned, grabbed menus, and led us to some tables outdoors. We thanked her and settled in as she disappeared to handle the rest of the crowd.

We were grateful for our table outdoors but didn't think much about it until later in the meal when our hostess came back to see us.

"I just wanted to say thank you," she began. "Since we opened today, the restaurant has been painfully busy. People waiting in line have been demanding, grumpy, and some of them demeaning. You have been so kind to me, the first people to smile at me all day. Thank you!"

She smiled and handed me a slip of paper.

"Next time you come, call me in advance. I would be happy to reserve a place for you." And she slipped back into the crowded restaurant.

We were stunned. All we did was smile, make a request, and choose to not demand our own way. But she felt valued by our simple gesture and it changed her day. Value is not difficult to create.

Stewards release peace where chaos and stress typically are found. We are generous when the atmosphere is greedy and stingy. We offer gentle words when wrath is expected. The world tries to squeeze the life out of us, and what comes out is love. These are a just a few ways among millions how stewards bring heaven's resource to earth and create value.

How do we *stay* connected to earth? We live in our unique identities given to us by God. We intentionally ground ourselves in our measures of rule, recognizing that we are given places of authority on earth to extend the Kingdom of God. The steward has discerning vision to see the truth of what is happening around her and is not distracted from the glory she carries or its purpose to heal the world around her.

We keep the pipeline flowing into the realm of earth by serving one another. We serve by exerting energy and resources to meet the needs around us. When we take upon ourselves the nature of a servant, we begin to understand something of the incarnation, that God became man and lived as a servant among us. Being a servant is core to the entire job description of the Kingdom steward (Philippians 2:1-11).

## 3. Creative Connections

Stewards do not operate independently. We have been created by God with strategic apportionments from heaven that require relationship with other stewards. Every relationship, every encounter, becomes an opportunity to receive and give revelation and understanding. The Kingdom friendships we have are bursting with dreams and possibilities. They carry the potential to spark divine revolutions on earth that bring transformation.

Even the language of the New Testament shows the inherent connection of stewardship with our relationships. Most of us have heard the word "koinonia," which we recognize as the New Testament word for fellowship. It speaks of a partnership, coming out of a word which literally means "sharers."[34] As distributors, we are sharers, and that which we share is multidimensional. Spiritual grace and gifts, in their multifaceted forms, are freely given to serve each other (1 Peter 4:11). We share physical resources such as food and money with one another, as the early church demonstrated in Acts 3 and 2 Corinthians 9:12-15.

Recall the house, or *oikos*, of God. We are the *oikonomos*, stewards of the house who administrate (*oikonomoi*). Stewards build up the value of the house by finding ways to edify one another (*oikodomeo* verb). (The italicized words in these scriptures are English translations for the Greek word *oikodomeo*—to build.)

"But everyone who prophesies speaks to men for their *strengthening*, encouragement, and comfort" (1 Corinthians 14:3).

"Let us therefore make every effort to do what leads to peace and to mutual *edification*" (Romans 14:19).

"Knowledge puffs up, but love *builds* up" (1 Corinthians 8:1b).

"Therefore encourage one another and *build* each other up, just as in fact you are doing" (1 Thessalonians 5:11).

Spiritual gifts are multifaceted in their beauty and expressions. These gifts are to be used with wisdom to edify one another (see 1 Corinthians 14) and even to build up or strengthen ourselves (1 Corinthians 14:4). Stewards receive these gifts from God and distribute them strategically as the Holy Spirit instructs them.

God partners with us, empowering us by His Spirit while allowing our unique voices and personalities to demonstrate His power with bursts of brilliance. When mature sons and daughters choose to exercise gifts and resources from God in agreement with Him, that act or word contains a power, an anointing, that has an impact much stronger than anything the enemy can do or say. "One sets a thousand to flight!" declares Joshua (23:10). Imagine what can happen when two or more are gathered, building each other up, operating in their measure of authority according to the grace given them through Jesus Christ. "Two set ten thousand to flight!" The power is multiplied as we join in fellowship, sharers in the power and resource of God. No wonder the enemy flees when believers exercise their authority and inheritance with confidence and faith.

We must keep our spiritual radars on alert for connections that God gives us with other stewards. This is a season in which we must establish powerful coalitions with people across the nations, building relationships with uniquely powerful stewards who are designed to release heaven's resources. You are created to dispense brilliant gifts that others need. Keep track of what is in your storehouse so you are ready to distribute it. Those you are in intimate fellowship with, and others you have distant connection with, likewise have resources essential for the building up of this house of God. These are "creative connections" because we get to partner with God in creating this house, designing and building these living stones together in a way that will honor Him.

He does not treat me like an inanimate "pipeline," dispensing the goods and services of heaven through me like plumbing with no choice. God honors you and me, letting us choose what treasure to release, when to release it, how and to whom. Sometimes we get the timing wrong. Sometimes we introduce elements of our own opinions that muddy the waters. But God wants us to learn from each opportunity. He is patiently and steadfastly training us how to walk in the Spirit and disperse His gifts with wisdom for maximum Kingdom impact.

# 7

## Economic Warfare

*"There is no neutral ground in the universe. Every square inch, every split second is claimed by God, and counterclaimed by Satan."*[35]

The house of God is at war. Principles of the household are fundamentally opposed by the kingdom of darkness. Greed and covetousness fight against generosity. Lust, pride, and deception seek to pilfer the house of its truth-treasures, hiding righteous weapons from stewards weakened by the grip of darkness. Identities become clouded. Inheritances are obscured by time and lies, and stories of hidden treasure fade like children's fairy tales.

Shake yourself to attention, steward! There is a war being fought over the house of God. You and the assignments you have been chosen to administrate are under attack. Heaven's treasures found within your measure of rule are enough to destroy plans of the enemy that took decades, even centuries, to set in place. You have the opportunity to inflict decimating losses on the enemy. The stewards of God are enforcing the Master's justice by exercising the authority and dominion legally given to them.

God intends for His treasures to be distributed on earth and the Kingdom of heaven extended to the nations. But there are anti-kingdom strategies of another household, a completely "other" economy, which directly oppose God's house.

Stewards must be aware of schemes that seek to attack or undermine the Kingdom's economy. Paul recognized the desire of Satan to outwit him, but the apostle knew that something as insidious as unforgiveness could play into the devious agenda of the enemy (2 Corinthians 2:11). Paul chose to forgive, releasing love toward the man who sinned against the body of Christ.

Jesus knew the character of the enemy. "The thief comes only to steal and kill and destroy" (John 10:10a). These objectives of the thief strike at the heart of any economy. With malicious intent his agenda is aimed at the heart of the Father. The enemy sneaks in to kill dreams and destroy everything in his path. His hatred burns against humanity, seeking to demolish Kingdom ministries, families, and marriages, all life itself. What he cannot kill, he seeks to ruin utterly, bringing destruction and pain, hoping to entice those who will join him in cursing God.

Since we know the truth about the enemy's objectives, we need to be aware of his methodology particularly as it applies to economics. Paul says to the Ephesians, "Finally, be strong in the Lord and in His mighty power. Put on the full armor of God so that you can take your stand against the devil's schemes" (Ephesians 6:10-11). In this instance, Paul uses a word related to *methodos*, meaning "with a road." It has the nuance of being a "way" that is cunning, full of trickery, and crafty. The word "scheme" in 2 Corinthians 2:11 is *noemata*, meaning a deceived mind. The enemy's method really revolves around "one road"—the pathway of deceiving the mind of man until the heart is hardened and a stronghold is formed.[36]

In spiritual warfare, the first battleground is the mind, requiring that we live the crucified life, transformed by the renewing of our mind (Romans 12:1). These schemes are attacks against heaven's goods and services, against the consumers themselves, and against distribution. Beyond knowing the enemy's schemes, we are able to take back what the enemy has stolen and rebuild or resurrect that which the Father has intended from the beginning.

## Attacking Heaven's Treasures

From the beginning Satan has sought to defile everything related to the house of God. Evil hates humankind almost as much as it hates God Himself, for we are created in the image of the Creator. Satan's aim is to turn humanity against God, the Creator and Source of every "good and perfect gift" (James 1:17).

You have seen the commercials that cast doubt on a competing product or directly oppose a candidate for political office. In the same way, the enemy seeks to defile the product and service of heaven through attack advertising. When the enemy begins to assault it from many sides, the consumer becomes confused or uncertain about miracles or gifts. They may question a prophetic word or doubt the possibility of financial provision. "That can't be from God," we hear. "God doesn't do miracles today." We feel the scorn in people's voices if we are vocal about the gift we have received. Intimidation comes from many sides.

Another way the enemy attacks heaven's treasures is by mixing error with truth. Language and Christian symbols in our culture dilute the truth, deflating truth-treasures into two-dimensional mantras to be hung on the refrigerator. "I believe" is sprinkled with doubt. The cross becomes a decorative piece, or a necklace best kept hidden so as not to offend or to attract the label of intolerance. "Spirituals" become cultural songs rather than expressions of worship. Hallelujah becomes a chorus instead of a rambunctious explosion of praise.

The kingdom of darkness attacks the products and services of heaven by marketing products that are "must have" imitations, counterfeits that have less upfront costs. Addictive and destructive, these counterfeits appeal to the flesh of man. Pulling upon our desire for wealth, gambling has been legalized and legitimized as a funding source for our education systems. Time, a crucial resource in God's economy, is siphoned away from pursuing God and His Kingdom as we pursue a countless variety of "must do" necessities.

Not all counterfeit products and services flooding the market of humanity appear dark. Even the fruit of the tree of the knowledge of good and evil looked good and pleasing. People are doing wonderful things, volunteering time, giving money, and offering compassion. Even churches can operate in the fruit of the "knowledge of good." Movements, groups, and individuals can have the appearance of godliness, complete with a cross to lend a stamp of approval. But many lack the power of the Holy Spirit and the authentication of the character of Father. "(M)ark this," Paul said, "there will be terrible times in the last days. People will be lovers of themselves, lovers of money, boastful, proud, abusive, disobedient to their parents, ungrateful, unholy, without love, unforgiving, slanderous, without self-control, brutal, not lovers of the good, treacherous, rash, conceited, lovers of pleasure rather than lovers of God—having a form of godliness but denying its power. Have nothing to do with them" (2 Timothy 3:1-5).

The enemy stops at nothing to attack heaven's treasures. False prophetic voices attempt to drown out the true prophet. Healings are dismissed as fanciful or relegated to the power of the human mind. The attacks are fierce and relentless.

## Attacking Consumers

The enemy wars against the intended recipients of God's infinite goodness. He turns these would-be consumers against the very gifts of heaven they long for, especially the gift of salvation. Principalities and powers of darkness work to cause humanity to reject the Giver of every good and perfect gift, abandoning Father, Son, and Holy Spirit.

The schemes are relentless. Make them spiritually blind and deaf, ignorant to the products and services of heaven. Market alternative truths in clever packaging. Use marketing campaigns with demonic anointings to brainwash the consumer. Keep them listless and indifferent, addicted to counterfeits. Redefine reality. Call what is good "bad," and what is evil "good." Convince them their sickness is a good thing—God's "merciful" tool to teach them a lesson. Feed their self-centered passions—help them indulge in their fantasies, and then yank their chain to torment them when the hook is set and their slavery is complete. Demean their identity, devalue their contributions. In short, kill the consumer. The thief comes only to destroy. *Utterly.*

Even within the church, as well-intentioned as we might be, we have definitions and declared values that actually *devalue* the identity of the consumer. For example, "humility" is twisted into debasement and groveling, rather than agreement with the affirmation of God. "Poverty" for some has become a badge of virtue. People destroy one another, fueled by hell's hatred. Christians attack Christians with bitter gossip and ranting diatribes from pulpits. "Meekness" is a mealy milk-toast imitation of the powerful Christ that leaves a bad taste in the mouth of the consumer. Whatever happened to believers as the salt of the earth, creating hunger and thirst for God and His Kingdom?

One of the most insidious doctrines raging against creation is that of Gnosticism. It is an old enemy, still exercising great influence in the church. It elevates the ethereal over the physical. This mindset is actually more Buddhist than Christian. It generates disdain for the physical universe, including our bodies. It is an affront to the Creator, who called all of creation good. Jesus Himself was raised by the power of the Holy Spirit, overcoming death in a tangible, physical resurrection. God has affirmed our physical existence as part of the full salvation that we have inherited. He has provided not only divine health on earth, but also a physical resurrection. Our future inheritance is not an ethereal, ghostly existence. We will be raised with Christ in real bodies, clothed in brilliant glory!

The enemy's assault against heaven's treasures and its consumers is insidious. Yet some of the fiercest battle plans of Satan are launched against one key component of the economy of God: Distribution.

## Attacking Distribution

God's treasures are making their way toward consumers who are in desperate need of answers. But the enemy rages against distribution and the distributors vehemently.

Consider the birth of Moses. Moses' measure of rule included delivering the people of God from the oppressive rule of Egypt. This possibility terrified the pharaohs. Every son born to a Hebrew mother was ordered thrown into the Nile River, executed by drowning or given as food for wild beasts. Moses was rescued, however, and became the principal conduit of freedom for the Hebrew people. As fiercely as Satan opposed Moses, even greater was the grace given to the son of both Hebrews and the pharaoh by God. Miracle after miracle accompanied this initially reluctant deliverer. As a distributor of the treasures of heaven, Moses not only delivered the children of Israel from slavery, but he also received the Ten Commandments and was entrusted with the blueprints for the tabernacle of worship. Moses was a faithful steward.

At the birth of Jesus, Satan sought the destruction of the promised Messiah through the same sweeping proclamation by a paranoid ruler, King Herod. Every male child under two years of age in Bethlehem and the surrounding regions was slaughtered. But through a dream, Joseph was warned to leave quickly with his young family. Jesus escaped the seething hatred of the enemy seeking the Messiah's premature death. And He continues to distribute salvation, grace, and all the treasures of heaven today and for all eternity.

The legalization of abortion fits this pattern today. This evil has tried to silence those destined to release heaven's treasures and deliver nations from the oppression of the evil one. These diabolical deaths may be convenient for Satan presently, but he is faced with a most inconvenient problem. The children of God, stewards of the treasures of heaven, are becoming an irrepressible force of righteousness and justice. Wickedness *will* be overthrown. Jesus *will* reign over the nations of the earth. Every knee *will* bow, and every tongue *will* confess that Jesus Christ is Lord (Philippians 2:10).

A crucial example of the enemy's opposition to the distribution of a treasure of heaven is in the Old Testament book of Daniel. The prophet and statesman Daniel was greatly disturbed about a vision he had received concerning a future war. He fasted, mourning over what he had seen.

After three weeks, while he was walking with a group of men by the Tigris River, a brilliant man appeared to him, an angel of the Lord (see Daniel 10). The angel spoke to Daniel about the process of delivering the message: "Do not be afraid, Daniel. Since the first day that you set your mind to gain understanding and to humble yourself before your God, your words were heard, and I have come in response to them. But the prince of the Persian kingdom resisted me twenty-one days. Then Michael, one of the chief princes, came to help me, because I was detained there with the king of Persia. Now I have come to explain to you what will happen to your people in the future, for the vision concerns a time yet to come" (Daniel 10:12-14). The angel was in a heavenly battle, opposed by forces of darkness from delivering the message to the prophet Daniel. Even the distribution pipes of angelic delivery are under attack by the enemy.

We can benefit by examining these examples of how the enemy attacks the distribution of heaven's treasures. As faithful stewards, we will become wise and effective in our management and delivery of these vast resources. Here are a few examples of how the enemy opposes Kingdom distribution.

***Blocked Transportation Routes:*** Jacob had a dream of angels ascending and descending between heaven and earth. The Lord Himself stood above it and declared the inheritance of land for Jacob and his offspring, promising that "all peoples on earth will be blessed through you and your offspring" (Genesis 28:14-15). After he woke up, Jacob said, "How awesome is this place! This is none other than the house of God; this is the gate of heaven" (v. 16). He built an altar and called the place Bethel, which means "the house of God."

Access points. Portals. Hot spots. Gates. Doorways. There are different words or phrases used by Christians past and present to describe places such as this where there is activity of "angels descending and ascending." The enemy is passionate to defile these transportation routes, these portals of distribution. Lou Engle, in his book *Digging the Wells of Revival*, makes a strong case for discovering the historical places of God's outpouring. The sins of men gave permission for the enemy's access. But by repentance the obstacles that plugged up the "wells" are removed. The glory of God is released once again in those places.[37]

What might be preventing heaven's resources from getting to God's people in your neighborhood, your city, or your region? Ask God. He will show you.

I woke up one morning hearing one word: *Interdict*. It was not part of my normal vocabulary, so I knew the Holy Spirit was speaking to me. At the time several people were preparing for a strategic prayer and warfare initiative in our region. We knew that God was exposing strategies of the enemy and preparing to release glory. I was not prepared for the impact of this word of knowledge.

I had to research its meaning to understand the implications. "Interdict: 1. A Roman Catholic ecclesiastical censure withdrawing most sacraments and Christian burial from a person or district. 2. A prohibitory decree. Also: 1. To lay under or prohibit by an interdict. 2. To forbid in a usually formal or authoritative manner. 3a. To destroy, damage, or cut off (such as an enemy line of supply) by firepower; to stop or hamper an enemy. 3b. intercept."[38]

As Holy Spirit began speaking to me, I began to understand much of the strategy and method of the enemy against the Kingdom of God in our city and region. First, He showed me how the religious and antichrist spirits had been working to cut off the Spirit-filled churches from grace and the anointing. A strong decree had been issued over our region by people agreeing with the enemy that empowered the barrier. Those who came into our valley to lead churches and ministries historically found themselves facing weariness, high levels of discouragement, and tremendous opposition. Businesses led by strong believers seemed to trudge through concrete, trying to make it financially. In some churches, preachers who began to preach on the Holy Spirit were removed. Any leader walking in the anointing of Holy Spirit came under significant attack. We had personally been the object of many of these attacks.

The Spirit then showed me how the enemy had come behind the lines of the Church to destroy, damage, or cut off supply by firepower, especially the churches that pressed into the grace and anointings of the Spirit of God. Particularly, we saw most of the Spirit-filled churches attacked in their finances, moral failure in leaders, broken relationships, defilement in prophetic ministry—the list goes on. We saw areas in the history of the Church in our region where sin had given ground to the enemy. Decisions were made within churches that quenched Holy Spirit. Early ministers in the city partnered in greed, theft, and gross abuse of Native Americans. We felt the fear of the Lord as a church and knew we needed to identify in repentance for many things the Spirit showed us in our research.

A few weeks later we were strategizing the places to which the Holy Spirit was leading us. In one of those locations, we were led to a tower where demonic proclamations were being released—seven days a week, twenty-four hours a day. The enemy was broadcasting a nonstop interdict against the Church in our region!

We discovered the sources of the enemy's power and strategy to cut off supply from the Ekklesia in our region. Through prayer and prophetic acts and spiritual warfare, we are beginning to realize the strength of the blessings of God and breaking the power of the enemy. In discovering the strategy of the enemy, we were able to interdict the enemy's own supply line.

*Hide Resource Storage Facilities:* Another scheme used by the enemy, and used quite effectively, is to hide the treasure rooms from view. This tactic is used to keep stewards blinded to their identity and inheritance. Once stewards know who they are and what their inheritance is, the enemy seeks to keep them from gaining access to the resources of heaven. It is a significant place of warfare in the heavenlies, trying to keep stewards blind to the reality beyond the curtain of the physical.

Prophecy is a clear revelation or insight from God to encourage, build up, or comfort people (1 Corinthians 14:3, 6). Do you need resource to build or to complete your assignment? A prophetic word is meant to reveal where to gain the resources or tools necessary for building. Even the word "revelation" in the Greek (*apocalupsis*) means the unveiling or uncovering. That which is hidden is revealed.

In the book of Revelation Jesus said to the church in Philadelphia, "These are the words of him who is holy and true, who holds the key of David. What he opens no one can shut, and what he shuts no one can open. I know your deeds. See, I have placed before you an open door that no one can shut" (Revelation 3:7-8). God places doors before us that allow us to access God's Kingdom and all that it has to offer.

Your word is your weapon. We stand at the door to our fields of influence. We use our key to shut out lack, fear, sickness, and discouragement. We use the key to throw wide open the door to the King of Glory, resource, courage, health, and faith.

**Attack Distributors:** The enemy's tactics are numerous. Oppose stewards through shame, ignorance of identity, generational sin, and unbelief. Exploit weakness, and feed on any unresolved flesh issues. Convince them they are not qualified to distribute such priceless treasures. Keep them feeling fearful and inadequate so they are caught in an eddy, constantly consuming. Distribution will not happen through Christians who simply resign themselves to being sponges for the swamp water of constant teaching. We must resolve to step out and do something with what we have received, for the sake of the Kingdom of God.

Other stewards have a distorted view of the delivery system, something the enemy is all too happy to reinforce. There is a nebulous, undefined sense that God, in His sovereignty, is going to ship the grace-gifts to them. "If God wants to give me the gift of tongues, He will." They wait passively, not realizing that the gifts are already available, and we are responsible for picking them up and using them.

I remember the stunning provision of God's grace in my life when I was newly empowered and set apart by the Holy Spirit. After thirty years of struggling in my own power to please God, I was amazed that He would trust me with such powerful gifts! During one encounter with God, I was shown a trap the enemy had laid for me to destroy me and the ministry the Lord had given us.

In a vision I saw an event that we would be attending in a few days. The expressed purpose of this gathering of Christians was to participate in an Agape Feast. The intent was to declare our love for God and one another and affirm our unity in Christ. Holy Spirit showed me unexpected twists, where the speaker began to denounce me and make public accusations against me. This man invited me to come to the pulpit to respond to the accusations. In the vision, I saw this unfold as if I were seeing through the eyes of God. A strong demonic spirit was standing at the front of the sanctuary waiting for me, a religious spirit. I was aware of its intent to pick me up and throw me against the front wall, to effectively destroy me publicly. But God's presence filled me; none of this caused fear in me as the vision unfolded. I was completely confident that God was with me, and that He had a solution. Then Holy Spirit whispered to me, "I will tell you what to say."

When the event happened a few days later, I had complete confidence that God would win, and the enemy would lose. All of it happened just as the Lord had shown me. But Holy Spirit gave me what to say, words that upended the enemy's scheme. God won; the enemy lost. Accusation melted under the force of forgiveness, and strongholds of bitterness were weakened. On that day, as difficult as it was, more of the goodness and glory of the King was deposited in His Kingdom in our region.

The solution did not just come to me. I had to go and access it. I put myself in a position to receive it by worshiping God that morning. I was in a place of offering myself to God, praising Him for His grace and goodness and kindness. His presence filled my living room as my praise pressed the thin barrier between heaven and earth. Like the 120 disciples gathered in the upper room, my waiting was neither passive nor powerless. I was waiting for His promises even as I actively pursued God. It is possible to reign in a place of authority as an honored son until the release of the promise.

Another way the enemy attacks God's distributors is to discredit them and the treasure God entrusted to them through sin. The enemy attempts to defile the distributor to discredit both the treasure and God. He gains access through pride, self-indulgence, and a myriad of temptations. We have all witnessed the impact of sexual sin, divorce, gossip, theft, and prejudice on churches, businesses, and government. Credibility sours, momentum is lost, and many times destinies are hijacked.

Through inadequacy, stewards can give out of the wrong "storeroom." Pride motivates the gift and it is broadcast with fanfare, like pharisaical alms. Giving simply out of duty rather than genuine love and generosity adds nothing to the economy of God's kingdom.

We attempt to build on to God's house with our programs according to our needs and ambitions or values. But anything birthed by the flesh instead of by the Spirit does not receive grace. Rather, it must be sustained by the energy of the flesh. Beware the imminent burnout. I remember the obscure hymn sung at my ordination service, "Burn Out for Jesus." I am sure the intent was to encourage us in our covenant to serve God the rest of our lives, but it sure didn't build me up at the time. Wood, hay, and stubble are works of the flesh, and they will burn. Silver and gold, however, remain as testimony of the purity and beauty of the treasures of God on earth, as it is in heaven.

What gifts has God blessed you with? Excel in them. Don't allow insecurity convince you that you must be like "so-and-so" to be effective in your assignment. Your business carries your divinely empowered DNA.

Manufacturing a program or identity just because it is currently trending will require your constant attention and energy. You will not have the invigorating presence of God to provide fruitfulness. Instead, the fire of His presence will test it. Only that which is from His storehouse will remain. You are a powerful distributor of God's treasures, not a trafficker of cheap, useless products.

*Attack Management:* There are many among us whom God has appointed as chief stewards, responsible for shepherding churches, businesses, cities, schools, studios—leaders in every group imaginable. These stewards carry tremendous responsibility. Five-fold leaders (apostles, prophets, evangelists, pastors, teachers) oversee gatherings of many sizes. They are tasked with protecting and encouraging, discipling and feeding, directing and managing resources crucial to the Kingdom of Heaven. These management teams are crucial in the Kingdom of God, and they are under attack.

Effective distribution systems require strong management teams with clear vision and leadership. They must have knowledge, understanding, and wisdom to make decisions. These teams must have flexibility both to operate in shifting roles, and to train and release people around them. It takes a remarkable leadership team in the Ekklesia to be effective and productive as faithful stewards. The hatred of the enemy wars against the Ekklesia operating in unity and in the power of the Spirit.

As a pastor, I have some experience in recognizing when management is under attack. Needs and desires that are not submitted to the King become food for the enemy. The accuser of the brethren is effective in his warfare, undermining authority, leading to betrayals and division. Leaders fall prey to idolatries that people have of them. A pedestal makes for good target practice. Don't be the one standing on it.

Chief stewards find themselves fighting temptation. People around them gossip and malign them. Jealousy is stirred up. Sauls seek to kill Davids, and Absoloms conspire to overthrow them. No one said being a chief steward would be easy. But the reward is great.

## Taking Back Our Distribution Rights

As sons and daughters of the Father we have the right to distribute the treasures of God on earth. We get the privilege of spending our inheritance here and now. Poverty is not a virtue and our inheritance is not just for a fanciful future life. Now is our time as stewards of the house of God, managers of the resources of the King, to begin distributing the treasures generously, lavishly, and wisely.

Take back your distribution rights stolen by the enemy. Repent of apathy and passivity. Worship God with all your might. Engage in thanksgiving and praise. Rejoice continuously. You will find yourself having less time for grumbling and complaining. You will be too busy testifying about what God has done!

Stewards have their eyes fixed on the Giver of good gifts. It is a powerful truth that we become what we behold. We become givers of heaven's treasures. We stand in the gap, interceding for intersections between heaven and earth. We pray and release harvesters into the fields. We are not afraid to engage in self-denial and fasting because we know we are coming into alignment with the plans and purposes of God.

As stewards of God's house, take back your distribution rights and move in the opposite spirit of the enemy. Don't lose the flow of heaven's treasures by reacting to the enemy's schemes with his tactics and disfigured character. When the enemy bites with hatred, we choose love. When he steals from us, we sting the enemy through our increased generosity. "You're going to steal from me? Ha! I will just give more away to feed the poor. That'll teach you to steal from the steward of God's house!" As I have heard Graham Cooke say often, we must absolutely wear the enemy out. If every attack against us results in God receiving glory and honor and praise, the limited resources of the enemy are going to have to be shifted somewhere else.

Stewards step into their distribution rights when they take inventory of the house. How can I give something away if I am not aware it exists and that I have the authority to distribute it? Go into the house of the

Lord. Take inventory of all the stored-up goods and services that He is granting you access to. Be ready to retrieve it, receive it, and give it away when the time comes.

Consider the story of Elijah and the widow in 2 Kings 4.

"Tell me," asks the prophet, "what do you have in your house?"

"Nothing at all," she replies, a bit blinded by her need. "OH! Except, a little oil."

If it is a little portion in the realm of man's ability, it seems insignificant; just, "a little." But a little portion on earth, seen from the perspective of heaven by a steward of the house of God, can easily be multiplied. Jar after jar after jar can be filled from just "a little." A little lunch from a boy becomes a feast for thousands in the economy of God. A mustard seed of faith moves massive mountains.

Stewards of the treasures of God do not chase after problems. They offer solutions. Otherwise we let the enemy set the agenda for "House Management" through the tyranny of the urgent. Sons and daughters of the King set the agenda for distributing heaven's treasures for our own assignments. When stewards begin distributing according to the wisdom and authority given them by God, they exhaust the enemy. Evil cannot keep up with the devastation to the kingdom of darkness caused by our stewardship and our weapons of warfare.

Such is the vengeance of the steward. Rather than struggling to keep things from falling apart, our inheritance and vision are shifting to a Kingdom that can never be shaken. Rather than getting stuck in an accusation echo chamber, struggling to change our attitudes, we go on the offensive and shift atmospheres with blessing. Instead of living from an impoverished view of our flesh, we live in the generous wealth of the King of all Kings.

Kingdom stewards are pulling heaven's treasures into this realm. We are transforming this world with heaven's possibilities. We have been learning to live by the principle of Maximum Kingdom Impact.

Are you ready to steward the house of God? Get ready for warp speed. Engage!

# 8

## You Look Just Like Your Dad

*"The Son is the radiance of God's glory and the*
*exact representation of his being, sustaining all*
*things by his powerful word" (Hebrews 1:3).*

If you haven't seen Jesus lately, He's beaming, just like His Father. The essence of the Son radiates the fullness of the Father. "Anyone who has seen me," Jesus said, "has seen the Father" (John 14:9). He resonates perfectly with the divine nature of the Father, even in flesh and blood. When his Father spoke, the man Jesus was in perfect unison with the waves of sound. Nothing in Jesus, whether spirit or soul or body, was on a contrary wavelength with a potential to cancel out or diminish the voice of his Father. Jesus was the "exact representation" of his Father.

The writer of the letter to the Hebrews used the Greek word *"charakteer"* for "exact representation."[39] The word referred to an image pressed onto a coin, or a ring worn by a king with a unique crest. The signet ring identified the king, his authority, and his ownership. Before an edict was sent out, the king would press his ring into clay or wax, signifying the source and authority of the proclamation. It bore the impress of the king, his *"charakteer."* The messenger and the message represented the king as if he were there in person.

When Jesus became a man, Father *was* the signet ring. Father pressed the fullness of Himself into His Son. "This is my Son, whom I love; with Him I am well pleased" (Matthew 3:17). Jesus did not simply bear the impression of God the Father; He became the exact image of the nature and person of God. His presence on earth carried the same impact as Father Himself being here.

In the book of Haggai, God said He would make Zerubbabel, a descendant of David, a signet ring (Haggai 2:23). The governor of Judah was a sign of the Kingship of God. Zerubbabel was himself God's stamp of authority upon His work of establishing the Kingdom on earth. As the governmental leader over the rebuilding of Judah, he was inseparably joined to the King, worn on the Royal hand of God like a valuable and outward sign to the world of His majesty and authority. His descendant, Jesus, would complete the work of redemption upon the earth. Through Him, the Kingdom would be established forever.

As the Son of God, Jesus bore the impress of His Father, the exact image of the nature and person of God. This is the privilege of the sons and daughters, to be conformed to the likeness of our Father. How do we know what God our Father looks like? We look at Jesus. Even though He was born sinless, Jesus chose every day to agree with the nature of His Father. He did this consistently throughout His life, even to the fullest extent of suffering and death.

Each of us was born into a sinful nature, and along the way chose to agree with it. Granted, that choice was often made in ignorance, but nevertheless, it opposed the nature of His righteousness. When we were born again, we were born into the righteousness of Christ. The old nature no longer had power over us. And thus began the process of character building. The impress of the identity and authority of God was beginning to be worked into our lives.

How God chooses to "impress" us is as unique as our fingerprints. The ways He disciplines me may not look like the ways He works His impression into you. Those who are parents or leaders understand the differences in discipline required. Lisa or I could simply look at one daughter and confront gently, and she would confess and repent wholeheartedly. With another, it required a more "hands on" approach. But transformations in character were just as real in each one.

**Producing Authentic Stewards**

Thanksgiving, worship, and intimacy with God shape my character. And so do meditating on scriptures, imitating godly men and women, and spending time in the wilderness. The list of tools God uses to produce mature, Christlike stewards is endless. One perhaps less familiar tool to produce character is suffering.

Paul makes no apology concerning suffering and its place in the life of the Christian steward. In several places he acknowledges his own suffering. In Romans 5, Paul writes:

> "Therefore, since we have been justified through faith, we have peace with God through our Lord Jesus Christ, through whom we have gained access by faith into this grace in which we now stand. And we rejoice in the hope of the glory of God. Not only so, but we also rejoice in our sufferings, because we know that suffering produces perseverance; perseverance, character; and character, hope. And hope does not disappoint us, because God has poured out His love into our hearts by the Holy Spirit, whom He has given us" (Romans 5:1-5).

Do you see God's economy in this? I admit I read this passage scores of times without seeing it. But when I started a business and began seeing life through the eyes of a steward and a growing understanding of economics, it dawned on me: Paul was describing economic multipliers in heaven's economy! Unpacking this in light of what we have previously seen reveals powerful treasures.

Let's begin with the word "access." It means to lead or bring toward. I refer to it as a "through-the-threshold" word. The key that unlocks that door is faith in Jesus Christ, and the treasure on the other side of the threshold where we now stand is grace (the empowering presence of God). Paul promises that there is hope for glory. It's not hard to see that glory is cause for rejoicing. "But so is suffering," says Paul! And this is why: Suffering carries within it the potential to boost production in the economy of God's kingdom. Welcome to the seemingly irrational economics of God!

Suffering produces perseverance, that dogged determination that will not let go regardless of the difficulties encountered. It is the pit bull tenacity of the Christian who sinks his teeth into loving his enemies like they were Jesus Himself. Despite the ridicule, vehement words, and bullying, he refuses to let go! Suffering becomes the "production facilitator," the factory that produces that necessary quality of perseverance. And to think, most of us avoid suffering like the plague.

Perseverance is in turn a factory. It produces trustworthiness, or character. Picture a piece of gold that has been through the crucible. The dross, the scum, the worthless elements have been forced to the surface and have been removed. The Assayer has assessed the gold, declaring it absolutely worth its weight. You can trust its worth as pure gold. It is deemed "Trustworthy." The impress of God's nature on a melted man is absolutely the mark of one who is trustworthy.

**Hope Does Not Disappoint**

Trustworthiness, or character, *produces hope*. And hope *does not disappoint*… I am absolutely captured by this hope! Paul knew this hope was more than a feeling. It was, and is, substantial. It is "Christ in you, the hope of glory" (Colossians 1:27). Like many English words, hope has lost its bearings from the original Christian confessions. Businesses capitalize on people buying products that provide "hope" for the future. As if buying the right toothpaste could make you attractive to the guys! Candidates for governmental office campaign on the promise of "hope," whether in economics, justice, or education.

That kind of "hope" offers little more substance than the Greek myth of Pandora's Box.

Pandora was the first woman, according to Greek mythology. She was sent by the gods to avenge the theft of fire by Prometheus. As a reward she was given a jar, or box, that was full of evils. She was told never to open it, but one day, curiosity got the best of her. Pandora opened the jar and unwittingly released all the evils into the world. But there was one thing that escaped Pandora's box that was not evil—*elpidzo*. It was hope. Hope, to the ancient Greeks, was nothing more than a silver lining on a very dark cloud. Impending doom in life is certain to crush the puny, powerless humans. But there was the smallest, most infinitesimal chance that something good *might* happen. But probably not. That was hope.

I have heard many Christians sound no different than the ancient Greeks: "I hope we survive this economic turmoil. I hope I find a job. I hope I can pay my bills. I hope we can somehow make it through this disaster." (Big shoulder shrug and a sigh.) "But it'll probably never happen."

The Christians of the early church changed the meaning of *elpidzo*. Hope to them was not the infinitesimal possibility of something good coming out of tragedy. They *redefined* hope, intrinsically tying it to faith and love. Hope became substantially real because of Jesus.

Hope is the impossible possibility, the exceeding abundance beyond imagination. Hope is the man Jesus, dead and buried, who flexed His identity and forever destroyed the bonds of death. Hope is flesh and blood resurrected to forever life. This hope is "an anchor for the soul, firm and secure" (Hebrews 6:19), not elusive or out there somewhere. This is true hope—change you can really believe in!

The progression from suffering to perseverance to character to hope is important. All humanity needs hope. "Hope deferred makes the heart sick" is a systemic truth (Proverbs 13:12). The consumers of the world need hope. Imagine if you could bottle it and take it out to the streets with the advertised guarantee, "Hope never disappoints!"

If you and I, as stewards of the resources of the house of God, are to distribute hope, it must be distributed as truth, not as an intellectual concept. I must *know* hope intimately, not just understand the theory. Distributing true hope requires that I have been to the production facilities of "suffering" and "perseverance." Otherwise, consumers will be skeptical. They have an innate capacity to do their own quality control. They are quick to recognize knockoffs, counterfeits that will not stand the test of their own need for truth.

Stewards distribute quality goods and services. Each product or service is stamped with the ring of the King, bearing the impress, the character of the King Himself. The stamp signifies to wary consumers, "This product is authentic. Trustworthy. It is produced by the son or daughter of the King. The goods you receive from their hands are genuine and have eternal value. The services they offer will launch you into inestimable life journeys." The authentic steward, "im-pressed" by the Master of the house, carries the King's authority and walks in the nature of the divine. Christian character is the exact representation of God.

He is love. Therefore, I am loved. Unbelievably, ridiculously, stupendously loved. I know who I used to be. Thoughts and attitudes inwardly betrayed my compliant, religious exterior. And the Father, my Father, drew me to Himself and loved me to life.

Do you remember being a child, and Dad or Mom held you on their lap, hugging you? Some kids are great at melting into Dad's embrace. Others squirm until they break free, anxious to do the next thing. You are not three years old anymore, but which one are you most like now, the snuggler or the squirmer? Examine the fruit of your life if you don't know.

The son or daughter who squirms when Father is around is a vastly different steward than the one who remains in His presence confident and joyful. We are His beloved children either way. But stewards are not simply offspring. They are disciples. The character of a disciple is formed either in intimacy *with* God or in our frenetic activity *around* Him. We can choose to accept His instruction or not.

## Kingdom Stewards Are Disciples

The disciples of Jesus are His followers. But that does not mean we just follow Him around from appointment to appointment, watching the Messiah do amazing things, and pat Him on the back. We don't say, "Cool! You're the man!" We are not tag-alongs, an entourage living off His fortune and fame. As His disciples, you and I are responsible for learning His words and His ways, living obediently to His commands. Stewards are not simply cheerleaders encouraging the Godhead; they are a family of lifelong learners putting into practice what they have seen in Jesus (see Luke 8:21).

Sons receive discipline. Hebrews 12:1-13 makes clear declaration that Father God disciplines us, His children. *"Our fathers disciplined us for a little while as they thought best; but God disciplines us for our good, that we may share in his holiness. No discipline seems pleasant at the time, but painful. Later on, however, it produces a harvest of righteousness and peace for those who have been trained by it. Therefore, strengthen your feeble arms and weak knees"* (Hebrews 12:10-12).

The little child (*teknon*) must be trained and disciplined by the Father into the character and nature expected of a mature son or daughter (*huios*). The one trained under this discipline becomes a mature adult to whom the Father entrusts responsibility and reward for the family business. They wear the signet ring of their Father.

The disciple is trained by discipline. And discipline requires that I step up and into submission to the Master. Muscles must be stretched and torn in order to produce more muscle. Going to the gym to work out is pointless if I stay within my comfort zone. I could bench press ten pounds, do it ten times, and call it a day. But I would never gain muscle. A trainer at my side would make sure I went beyond my comfort and felt the burn!

A steward's measure of rule will never be discovered in his comfort zone. Only a true disciple will be able to press beyond the easy chair of comfortable into greatness. Jesus said, "*I tell you the truth, anyone who has faith in me will do what I have been doing. He will do even greater things than these, because I am going to the Father*" (John 14:12). Do you hear the voice of the trainer here? Obedience to His commands demonstrate the disciple's love for Him.

"Even greater things than these" sounds wonderful to us. "Ooh, ooh, pick me, pick me!" we volunteer. I can imagine God the Warrior King of Heaven's Armies standing next to me. He puts a load of weights on either side of my barbell. "Tell me that you love me, soldier, and don't use words. Give me ten!"

All that to say this, simply: Stewards are *teachable*. To be teachable means we are "impressionable," hearts ready to receive the disciplines and teachers God sends us. The sons and daughters are *humble*, recognizing and agreeing with the voice of God through the simplest, most unlikely of teachers. Even through our harshest critics, we see Him at work disciplining us, using their words to chisel away our stone hearts to unleash the streams of the beauty of His likeness in us.

The mature steward is an *overcomer*. They "love not their lives, even unto death" (Revelation 12:11). The fiercest warrior on the field is the one who is not afraid of death. Like our older brother, Jesus, no threat, no intimidation, no overt action of the enemy will keep us from delivering the resources from heaven to earth. Stewards refuse to lick their wounds, navel gaze, or engage in any measure of self-pity.

## The Enemy Has Nothing in Me

Several years ago I recall praying a phrase with a bunch of friends who were passionate after the heart of God. This remains a statement of vision and overcoming for me: "*Nothing to hide, nothing to lose, nothing to fear, nothing to prove*" (Ryle, n. d.). These, too, reflect the character of the steward.

"*Nothing to hide*" speaks of transparency and sincerity. Hidden sins, unconfessed, are handles by which the enemy can yank us out of our identity and our measure of rule. Many of my Christian brothers and sisters shrink back from their authority and calling because of hidden sin. The steward, by covenant, remains in the fire of Father's embrace, allowing His holiness to judge the sin within. Confession releases the hidden sin into the light, where it is destroyed and rendered powerless. When the steward has nothing to hide, she can go anywhere with confidence and boldness, even the throne of God (Hebrews 4:16).

Sincerity is a strong character quality of heaven's economists. It doesn't take a spiritual gift of discernment to recognize lack of sincerity, even in the church. The word sincere comes from two Latin words common during the time of Roman occupation: "sin" and "ceres."

Artists were plentiful in Roman culture. Sculptors were busy carving marble busts, profiles of the rich and famous, and statues of the gods. There was a big market for sculptures, and a good profit to be made. Like any business with excellent profitability, less reputable artists began selling marble busts and statues.

The careless sculptor would slip, chiseling off the nose, perhaps, or an ear. Fearful they would lose out on making a profit, they would fashion a piece of wax to mimic the marble nose or ear. The typical consumer could hardly tell the difference, until they took it home, placed it in the sun, and the nose melted off! The deceitful practice became so prevalent, reputable artists began hanging a sign on their sculptures: "Sin Ceres"—"Without Wax."

The steward of God is "without wax." They are not putting up a false image of themselves, hiding behind wax and religious makeup. When the steward makes a lavish distribution of love, it must be, as Paul says in Romans 12:9, "sincere." Then, when the sun comes up and the heat rises, the workmanship is revealed for what it is: genuine. This steward has nothing to hide.

"Nothing to lose" is about purity of heart. Jesus, teaching the crowds on the mountainside, released a series of blessings we refer to as the

"Beatitudes," recorded in Matthew 5:3-12. "Blessed are the pure in heart," he said, "for they will see God" (5:8). I appreciate the definition given by Soren Kierkegaard for purity of heart: *To will one thing.*[40] It is an undivided heart, not addicted to the lusts of the flesh, nor chasing after the baubles that catch our eye and capture our heart.

The rich young man in Matthew 19:16-30 had something to lose. He came to Jesus passionate about obtaining this eternal life he had heard about. The stumbling block came when Jesus told him, "Go, sell your possessions and give to the poor, and you will have treasure in heaven. Then come, follow me." Matthew records that "when the young man heard this, he went away sad, because he had great wealth" (19:21-22).

Many of us allow money and possessions to occupy a place in us that causes us to hesitate when the Master says, "Give." Faithful stewards give unflinchingly. Purity of heart gives clarity to vision. To steward the resources of the house of God, our eyes must be clear to see God, *now, not just future glimpses of heaven.* That is an integral part of the blessing of purity of heart.

We have many "idols" exposed when confronted with this test, not just money. Loss of family or friends, loss of reputation, loss of talent... the list is as long as the heart's capacity to covet or desire. The cross of Christ is our remedy. As we choose to die with Him, freedom comes to release us into unlimited possibilities. A dead man is not vulnerable to the enemy's threats to steal, kill, or destroy.

Similarly, "*nothing to fear*" speaks to the freedom and the capacity of the steward for love, generosity, and boldness. The enemy operates in the realm of fear, for we serve what we fear. The fact that we are afraid indicates idols that need to be overthrown. But the redeemed of the Lord fear only Him, no one and nothing else. Stewards do not fear death. We do not fear pain, suffering, humiliations—we are formidable warriors on the battlefield, relentless distributors of heavenly resources, and boldly unpredictable. What other army of warriors would dare sprint into the camp of the enemy armed with a towel and a cup of cold water?

When you have nothing to fear, the simplest treasures of God become destructive to the strongholds of darkness.

*"Nothing to prove"* testifies to the security, wisdom, and humility of the steward. When the driving need of a son is significance, he will do whatever he thinks he needs to obtain that acceptance and recognition. If he seeks his identity in anyone but Father God, he finds only insecurity. Restless, squirming out of the lap of God, and unfocused, the son tries to prove his worth. "Look at me. Value me. Love me." Father cannot trust him with more than a limited measure of the treasures. The steward in search of significance is at high risk of spending the treasure in an attempt to make himself look good.

King Hezekiah needed to show off the treasury of Jerusalem to the envoys from Babylon. "There was nothing in his palace or in all his kingdom that Hezekiah did not show them" (Isaiah 39:2). Perhaps Hezekiah sought significance. Why would Hezekiah expose the wealth of his nation, all the treasures amassed through previous generations' work and exploits? Was it to prove his significance? Or to impress foreigners? It worked. The visitors were impressed! It wasn't long before they invaded Judea and stole the entire wealth. Hezekiah's pride had calloused his heart so that he could no longer see the value of his family or the people he had endangered by his posturing. Most of all, his heart had become hardened to God and His judgments.

Hezekiah's chief of staff for a season was Shebna (Isaiah 22:15). As a chief steward of the king, Shebna had great responsibility and privilege. Isaiah points out that the royal steward had a tomb carved for himself in the rocks, essentially a tomb fit for a king. Shebna was removed from his position, a disgrace to his master's house (vv. 18-19). Perhaps the grasping for significance and the resultant pride of Hezekiah attracted leaders of the same character, or even reproduced them.

Humility, on the other hand, agrees with God concerning identity: "I am exactly who God says I am. I exist to please God, not man. Whether servant or king, employer or employee, my identity is secure in Him. I live from my identity in Him, not for an identity through the approval of others." The cloak of humility guards the godly steward from impetuous presumption. Wisdom is the humble man's tutor. The administrator of the house of God listens to Wisdom, discerning the best places to invest God's resources. "This seed will be fruitful if we plant it here. This land needs preparation. Give the bread to the poor; teach them as you feed them, and then when they are ready, show them how to plant."

The steward with "nothing to hide, nothing to lose, nothing to fear, and nothing to prove" is free to risk, free to explore, even free to get it wrong.

These are the economists of heaven who, because they have been faithful with little, are given much (Matthew 25:21).

"Blessed are the pure in heart, for they will see God." Believing, they see. And in seeing, they become just like Him. And being just like Him, no one can stop them from giving Jesus His full inheritance, not even the gates of hell. The enemy has nothing in them to feed on.

It is a brilliant plan, bride of Christ. We throw off every hindrance and run the race planned out in the mind of Christ. Our lives are impressed with the glory of the Risen One, and everywhere we go, darkness flees and life flourishes.

## Final Thoughts on Character

Just attaining the position and status of a chief steward is not the endgame. True stewards bear the divine nature and the "DNA" of God. Whether they own a business, lead a school, or serve in a respected governmental position, these sons and daughters are a new creation, carrying the Kingdom reality within them, "predestined to be conformed to the likeness" of Jesus, the firstborn (Romans 8:29). They are clothed in glory, empowered by grace, and they freely dispense the provision of that grace. When they ask that Father's Kingdom come to earth as it is in heaven, they are inviting Holy Spirit to flow through them, expecting to see the Kingdom made manifest. It is this likeness which sets the Kingdom steward apart to effectively distribute the graces of the house of God.

Allow Holy Spirit to highlight other qualities necessary for you to faithfully steward the resources of heaven. We serve others, whether believers in Jesus or not. We abide in Christ, bearing all the fruit of Holy Spirit to such measure that there is always enough love, joy, peace, patience, kindness, goodness, faithfulness, gentleness, and self-control to give away (Galatians 5:22-23). We are intentional and strategic, prepared by the logistics expert (Holy Spirit) for anything.

We possess focus and determination; we are not distracted nor discouraged by anything or anyone. We are generous beyond reason and expectant as though every moment were pregnant with God's treasures and purpose.

Thanksgiving is our language of choice. We enthrone the King of Kings with our praise. Grumbling and complaining are far from us. Blessings and honor flow from us like liquid gold. Integrity is inherent to our nature. Bribes don't move us. Manipulation and control have no effect upon us.

For we are sons and daughter of the King, stewards of the house of God.

# 9

## Chief Oikonomos

As I developed my business serving owners of beautiful, high-end homes, I was consumed with details and minutiae. Comprehensive spreadsheets for every house listed copious details of paint colors, maintenance protocols, subcontractors, and owner preferences. I kept calendars for inspections, repairs, and scheduled visits. Weekly examinations of exterior grounds and crawl spaces and mechanicals throughout the estates required that I stay alert to any possibility of necessary maintenance and planning for future development.

Those who are called to leadership in any realm of influence often lead in multiple areas of leadership. At times as chief steward I felt overwhelmed. I was stressed under the sheer weight of responsibility in my business. An amazing staff counted on me for provision. Then came the responsibilities as a husband and father. I still had to steward my own household! And if that wasn't enough, a gracious body of believers called me "Pastor."

Every Christian is a steward. Each one is given some portion of God's vast estate to manage, but not everyone is given responsibility to lead and provide for others. The one who is responsible for leadership of house staff and managing larger aspects of the house, or economy, of God is a chief steward, or chief *oikonomos*.

Much is required of a chief steward. The house of God is massive!

His economy encompasses realms both known and unknown. In the body of Christ, we are just now grasping the truth that He has given us dominion in His economy/house. We hardly have the capacity to grasp the scope of the estate, let alone all the responsibilities—and we are the *mature* sons and daughters!

So, let's step back from the Abyss of Impossible Details. Sit with me on the back deck of this great house on the hill. The morning sun is rising behind us, unwrapping the beauty of Father's estate. I want to point out a few things as you take in the vista and ponder stepping into your role as Chief Oikonomos.

You can see the town off to the right. The businesses and schools and houses growing toward the horizon. A river reflects the morning sun moving from somewhere close to us on the left, flowing through the land and past the city. Farmland with rich soil is ready for spring planting. And further south a stunning mountain range still blanketed with the winter and spring snows.

Can you see the light of His glory in the land? Look closely. It is more than natural beauty, though it includes that. Focus your faith-eyes that have matured in the presence of the Father. Look at buildings, and your faith will glimpse businesses under the grow-light of Holy Spirit's nurture and instruction. Homes and neighborhoods with Kingdom-minded men and women carry the light. Now look at some of the different plots of farm and ranch land. Some of them look like they manifest life and health. The light of Father's glory is radiating across the region.

Nations will come to this light. Kings will be drawn to the brightness of the dawn. The previous caretaker, our enemy, preferred thick darkness. As the "god of this age" he blinded the eyes of those who are yet to believe in the truth of the gospel of the Kingdom so they could not see the radiant glory of Jesus the Anointed One (2 Corinthians 4:4). The usurper conditioned our eyes for darkness. But as we believed in Jesus we began to see.

The fact that you can look out from this deck and see beauty means that you have moved past simple glimpses of glory and can see the details that testify to God's brilliance. Now you *believe* and you see with eyes tuned to glory. Those whose hearts are tuned into light will see the light grow with ever increasing glory. You see the darkness grow as well, but you no longer see it through the eyes of a victim. You see it as a strategist, with clarity, insight, and powerful weapons.

As you look out toward the horizon, you probably have a million questions. You were created that way as a chief steward. The Father who owns all this will be meeting with you, pointing out the places and resources and boundaries you need to know about. Be free to ask all the questions you want because He is your Father.

Jesus, our older brother, is out there amid the estate. The day is young, but you can see Him working with the young rancher over there, wiping His brow and pointing out a way to increase the land's yield in the coming years. Jesus already shouldered the heavy lifting to restore all creation to Father's design and intent. He is the Messiah. Our ability to rest in our work is based on His ability to finish what He started. Our work as stewards is not toil. We might sweat, get stretched beyond our limits, but even when we are tired, the work will ultimately prove fulfilling.

If you are serious about being a leader, responsible for stewarding portions of the economy of God, you must know the fundamental requirements of being a Chief Oikonomos.

**1. Know God.** It sounds simple, but you cannot start from any other place. As you look across the land, let it speak to you about who He is. Remember that He owns the estate. Discover His preferences. What does God value? Understand what is most important to Him.

In business we are used to looking at "the bottom line." But what does that mean if this is Father's business? A dynamic evangelist says, "It's all about souls!" An amazing worship leader says, "It's all about worship!" A teacher says, "Above all else we must get them grounded in the word of

God." Which is most important to the Father? It is good to understand and appreciate one another's hearts and the motivational gifts of so many other gifted leaders. Perhaps your answer to the "bottom line" says more about your own gift perspective than the broad picture of the full heart of God. Let God stretch your imagination to encompass the full landscape from Father's deck.

Examine His architecture. The way He designs and builds structures in the natural and the spiritual realms are insights into His own nature and character. For example, the book of Proverbs observes that Wisdom builds a house. Understanding provides the structure with strength and endurance. Knowledge fills it "with rare and beautiful treasures" (Proverbs 24:3-4). However, our culture of education turns this upside down. It claims that knowledge is the foundation, understanding gives it structure, and wisdom is the beautiful artwork that graces the halls.

God is actively building the house. Any attempt to build apart from Him is "in vain" (Psalm 127:1). Our confession of who Jesus is creates a foundation upon which *He* will build his Ekklesia (Matthew 16:18). You might build a business, or a family, or a fellowship of believers, but as you come into intimate knowledge of His heart, you will understand what He values and build together with Him.

I am beginning to understand as an apostle and entrepreneur that revelation is the starting place for everything I build. Only by accessing heaven's blueprint room will I discern a design that I will not have to build or sustain in my own strength. Revelation, or wisdom, is the starting place; understanding gives us further language and tools with which to build.

If you want to know the Father, devour the Scriptures. Spend time in His presence. Let the Spirit and the Word open your heart to see more and more of the glory of who He is.

**2. Know Who You Are.** Only when you know who you are do you walk in the fullness of your authority and power. Shame steals from you, keeping you from the boldness, courage, and freedom to fulfill your purpose. A chief steward must know she has permission to speak freely to the Father. That is part of what it means to come "boldly before the throne" in Hebrews 5:16. Then she will have the disposition of a warrior, able to take "a decisive stand against *(the devil)* and resist his every attack with strong, vigorous faith" (1 Peter 5:9, addition mine, TPT).

Remember Peter? If you confess who Jesus is, He will tell you who you are. He is the best one to make declaration of your identity. I remind you; God is your Father.

In fact, He is willing to join you on the deck right now. Ask Him what He loves about you, why He made you the way He did. Write every word that He says to you. Make it a declaration of your identity. Take every word He says and declare it daily.

**3. Define Your Measure of Rule.** You are not responsible to steward every detail, every field or building that you see. You are not the only Chief Oikonomos. Jesus has given grace-gifts to every believer, and we are in a beautiful symbiotic relationship. As each part of the body is built up, the whole house will be in unity and "experience the fullness of what it means to know the Son of God" (Ephesians 4:13, TPT).

Remember, your grace and empowerment operate within a metron, or a measure of rule (2 Corinthians 2:13). Discovering the boundaries of your own metron is especially important for you as a son or daughter operating with responsibility in Father's business. You have freedom to explore the boundaries. Test the fruit. Did you sense the empowerment of Holy Spirit even if it was difficult for you? Or were you exhausted and unfulfilled? Listen to the voice of Holy Spirit as you critically (and truthfully) examine the process. Let Him define the boundaries of your metron for you.

I am good at math. But whenever I felt responsible for the financial books of the household or business, I failed. Miserably. I learned to step back and let others do the bookkeeping and accounting. I still read the financial reports and make decisions, but there are better qualified stewards who handle the details.

Remember, it is God who sets your boundaries. He may have intention to teach you something within a specific metron for a season. As you mature your boundaries may increase. Or Father may want to shift your boundaries as your calling develops. Nothing you have learned or gained within that metron is lost or wasted. Your experiences in one metron have prepared you for the next.

Our measure of rule is where we discover our inheritance and the resource to fulfill our purpose. Outside that sphere, provision dwindles and can consume our focus. That is understandable when scarcity seems to prevail in the budget. The strong temptation is to look for provision elsewhere. As we stray outside our metron, we begin exchanging hours for dollars. We trade out meaning and purpose for money. For a season we are covered by God's mercy, but the demands of toil finally shake us into the realization: "I don't have grace for this!" When we get our eyes back on the Provider, He leads us back to our measure of rule. We find our land of inheritance once again and resource flows again.

Part of unlocking resource within our metron is seeing the horizon with the Father's eyes. When we see what He sees, the resource is unlocked because we walk with eyes saturated in faith and hope. He knows the plans He has for this land, and He gives His leaders a heart to see the harvest He is providing for and expecting. We see purpose. Our attention is captured by a bigger horizon of the truth of God's house: provision is not simply *produced* by Him or *distributed* by Him; it is ultimately *unto* Him. He gives us harvest eyes and releases rivers of resource that will cause the entire economy to flourish and bring glory *to* Him.

When you understand your metron, you will know your assignment. Then the mission, vision, and provision will become clear to you.

**4. Get Clarity.** Clarity is essential. Some would go so far as to say, "Clarity is power." I agree. When the masks of deception are cut away and the fog of confusion is dissipated, communication and action accomplish what is necessary.

The word of God cuts through resistance like a sharp, double-edged sword. It always goes out with power to accomplish His purpose. Another interpretation of the Greek word for a double-edged sword is a "two-mouthed" sword. It makes sense when we understand that God said it first, and then we give voice to the same word. It thrusts against the enemy like a double-edged sword. Anything in the way must yield to the force of His word expressed in your voice. No deception or confusion can withstand it. Use the word as a sword to cut through the murky cloud that keeps people in confusion and indecision.

As a Chief Oikonomos we are required to have vision. We see in part. There are seasons to engage and move full speed ahead toward an intended destination. Other times we may be in a holding pattern, circling above our destination, waiting as things are being prepared for the word to finish its work. All the while we keep our eyes on the target, engaged in preparations for the mission. Clarity provides the confidence to see the season, the staff assigned to us, and the harvest ahead of us.

**5. Create Value.** If I have learned anything from being a chief steward, I cannot stress this point enough: Your task as a steward is not to maintain the value of the estate, but to create value. Maintenance is important, make no mistake. A house can quickly lose value if a boiler is not fixed in the middle of winter and all the pipes freeze and break. Fail to inspect the foundation and an entire house can be condemned. Maintenance is necessary for maintaining value. But our assignment does not end there.

Jesus gave a crucial lesson in the parable of the talents. In Matthew 25, Jesus said that the kingdom of heaven "will be like a man going on a journey, who called his servants and entrusted his property to them. To one he gave five talents of money, to another two talents, and to another one talent, each according to his ability.... After a long time the master of those servants returned and settled accounts with them" (vv. 14-15, 19). The first two servants put the money to work and doubled it. "Well done, good and faithful servant! You have been faithful with a few things; I will put you in charge of many things. Come and share your master's happiness!" (v. 21).

The third servant buried the money and earned nothing except a harsh rebuke, including the words, "You wicked, lazy servant!" Have you considered that while the owner was on his long journey, he was paying for the living expenses of his servant? Likely, the servant ended up costing the owner more than the one talent he buried.

Whatever your assignment is, determine to create value. Serve beyond the level of maintenance. Be innovative and creative in your efforts to increase the value of the economy of God. I have discovered that the Son and the Spirit are happy to assist with your plans to bring increase to Father's house!

**6. Lead Others.** Life contains seemingly endless gaps. There is a gap between present and future, reality and dreams, problems and solutions, theory and praxis. True leaders have the capacity to clarify the present, translate a vision, and influence followers into a transformed reality. They provide a bridge from problem to solution, confusion to clarity, despair to hope. Whether it is leadership in a corporate boardroom that charts a course to health and profitability, or in a ministry context influencing individuals, groups, and regions from cultural darkness to Kingdom of heaven transformation, these leaders have the capacity and authority to bring change.

Servant leadership is an important leadership model. Ken Blanchard defines servant leadership as the leadership model of Jesus, and that its defining characteristic "means loving like Jesus."[41] The development and focus of the leader begin in the heart, then move to the head, the hands, and the habits.

However, a key problem in traditional servant leadership surrounds authority. Servant leadership agrees all authority stems from God, but there is so much fear of man's misuse of authority that they feel a strong need for strict accountability. Consequently, the servant leadership accountability model tends to inflict an overuse of authority, stripping the leader of his power to lead. But an authority that is given by man can be taken by man. Leaders will often be tentative and fearful, afraid that if they make a risky decision that "fails," they could lose their position. Leaders who are fearful will be slow to make decisions, and tentative in making transformational cultural shifts.

An additional weakness of the servant leadership model is the tendency to focus more on needs than on vision. The tendency is to be need-driven, Spirit-sensitive, rather than Spirit-led, need-sensitive. In Colossians 3:17, Paul says, "And whatever you do, whether in word or deed, do it all in the name of the Lord Jesus, giving thanks to God the Father through Him." It is difficult to be driven by the needs and dictates of man while trying to serve God.

A better leadership style is referred to as apostolic leadership. In apostolic reformation, apostles receive their right and authority to influence from God, not man.[42] Authority is a legitimate right to use power on behalf of others. A true apostle only functions under and with God's authority. They have both authority and power to influence and build the culture of the Kingdom of God.

Apostolic leadership affirms that authority comes from God, not man. It affirms that one should be Spirit-led and need-sensitive. The focus is building the Kingdom of God and bringing transformation to the nations. It is a big-picture perspective. And rather than being consumed with the daily servant leader checklist, the apostle hears and obeys the Holy Spirit and the Word and takes action toward the vision rather than being stuck wondering if he or she has the authority to go and do.

A core motivation of an apostolic chief steward is still to serve. When love fuels our passion, serving feels like a promotion and a privilege. But with all the serving, remember to lead. Your leadership is only imaginary if you are chasing the needs of those you think you are assisting. Then you are not leading. You are following. Your first allegiance is serving the Owner of the House.

Leading also requires readiness. Jesus addressed His disciples, "Be dressed ready for service and keep your lamps burning, like men waiting for their master to return from a wedding banquet, so that when he comes and knocks they can immediately open the door for him. It will be good for those servants whose master finds them watching when he comes..." (Luke 12:35-38). A posture of readiness requires our expectation for the Master's return and a store of supplies to sustain the House for a quick response.

Leading also means caring for the "staff" and providing for them. Peter wanted to know if Jesus was addressing the disciples (leaders) or everyone. "The Lord answered, 'Who then is the faithful and wise manager, whom the master puts in charge of his servants to give them their food allowance at the proper time? It will be good for that servant whom the master finds doing so when he returns. I tell you the truth, he will put him in charge of all his possessions'" (vv. 42-44). His commission for these leaders gave direction for distributing the *owner's* provision at the proper time. Caring for the people you are responsible for leads to the distinct reward of stewarding the property assets of the owner, whether it is in the context of your office at work or in a ministry organization.

I pastored a church where the financial structure established by the denomination allowed us to lower our budgeted funds owed to the regional and international church if we bought physical property. Many churches were incentivized to buy land or buildings to lower their budgets. As a leader I knew the needs of the people in our care. A new building would have been amazing! But as I prayed, I kept getting pulled toward adding more staff, people I knew to have beautiful servant hearts. We added the staff. Our denominational budgets remained high, plus we spent significantly more on salaries and benefits for the new staff.

The decision, however, resulted in blessing. More finances were added to the church than any year previously. Plus, the additional staff were multipliers of love and grace to the growing body of believers in our community. We prioritized the blessing and provision of God's people and saw a radical increase of God's possessions to steward.

If you are called to leadership, God has prepared and equipped you to be a chief steward. It is a great honor. In the years of your preparation, you have no doubt suffered loss, rejection, and accusation as the press of God's hand left the imprint of His nature on your character. You have learned to love well. At times you have felt the fire of His holy love, and other times the bewilderment of feeling God is a million miles away— but you kept trusting and believing. You discovered that He is serious when He says, "For those who have received a greater revelation from their master are required a greater obedience. And those who have been entrusted with great responsibility will be held more responsible to their master" (Luke 12:48, TPT).

Chief stewards who lead faithfully inspire the whole staff to manage God's house. Jesus said those who steward well will be given charge over cities. To those who are faithful with little, much more will be given. God Almighty has a brilliant purpose and an economy that will never experience a recession. Now is the time for you to rise up with confidence to take your place as Chief Oikonomos of His Estate.

# 10

## Economics in the "Real World"

*"They all ate and were satisfied"* (Matthew 15:37).

The Chief of all Stewards sat down on a hill overlooking the lake. He had just completed a fifty-mile journey from the north. The view was beautiful with dust and anticipation rising around Him. Huge crowds were streaming up the hill, bringing with them the blind, deformed, lame and so many others needing healing. The hopeful masses laid their family and friends in need at the feet of Jesus and He healed them all.

On that hill above the lake the festival atmosphere exploded with promise. For *three days* the crowd, consisting mainly of Gentiles, celebrated the miracles and praised the God of Israel. Jesus and His friends loved them and laughed with them and renewed a vision for their futures. Amid political and economic oppression, hope was ignited.

Remember the economic realities of the Middle East during the time of Jesus. Debt, tax, and tributes devastated the region for years. Land had been confiscated by the Romans and given to rulers, both political and religious. The previous owners became tenant farmers. They were required to give one-half of all crops to their new landlords. Exorbitant taxes led to poverty. Any unpaid taxes resulted in confiscation of what they had left. Resort city projects instigated by the Romans exacted tributes from residents and travelers. Loans were offered—at 50 percent interest. Extreme poverty and hunger were normal, "savings" were unheard of, and debt crushed the people, both Jew and Gentile. The Romans had effectively destroyed the community-based economy instituted by the laws of God in Israel, a formerly prosperous economy that blessed the surrounding regions.[43]

These people had not eaten in days, and some of them had journeys ahead of them for the return home. Hungry but happy, the celebrating crowd surrounded the Steward. Compassion gripped Him. He knew it was time to pull even more upon the storehouse of heaven's resources to meet a very practical, real-world need.

He called the stewards-in-training close and declared His desire: "I don't want to send them away hungry." In other words, "Boys, these ten thousand desperately hungry people need to be fed. Feed them."

The disciples ran a quick inventory when Jesus specifically asked how many loaves of bread were available. "Seven," they replied, "and a few *small* fish."

In God's economy, that was enough. The throng of the thankful feasted until "everyone was full and satisfied" (Matthew 15:37, TPT). In fact, such a huge supply of bread and fish were left over, it filled seven baskets. And these baskets were massive! They were man-sized, the same type used to lower a man named Paul over a wall several years later.

## Real-World Need

Fast-forward to the year 2020. It was chaotic, to say the least. Some might say apocalyptic. COVID-19 sparked fear of a pandemic with potential to devastate populations worldwide. Governments legislated mandatory isolation. Schools, churches, offices were locked up, restaurants and marketplaces shut down.

From the beginning, prognosticators appeared to align with a spirit of fear disguised as extreme caution. The economy felt immediate effect as more than twenty million Americans filed for unemployment benefits in one month's time. Some economists projected a particularly harsh permanent loss as 40 percent of all jobs shut down in the U.S. due to COVID-19.[44] The European Commission released its forecast in May 2020 that the Gross Domestic Product of the twenty-seven-country bloc, originally projected to grow 1.2 percent in 2020, was now looking at a loss of 7.4 percent. By comparison, the financial crisis in 2009 saw a loss of 4.5 percent. The Commission reported, "The current crisis has now pushed the EU into the deepest recession in its history and unemployment rates are set to spike."[45]

But the COVID-19 issue is just a small piece of the larger scale real-world economy. Worldwide, it is projected that nine million people die every year of chronic hunger and hunger-related diseases. In India, nearly 200 million people are undernourished. April 2020 estimates for global poverty were approximately 8.6 percent of the world. Those who live in extreme poverty live on $1.90 or less per day.[46]

Why is there so much poverty and suffering in a world with incredible knowledge and technology? Ed Silvoso contends that addressing poverty is a necessary issue and paradigm that today's church must address. "The elimination of systemic poverty in its four dimensions—spiritual, relational, motivational and material—is the premier social indicator of transformation. 'The Spirit of the Lord is upon Me, because He anointed Me to preach the gospel to the poor' (Luke 4:18)."[47] As chief stewards, managers of this household called earth, our task is the proclamation and demonstration of the good news of the Kingdom of God that invites nations into real transformation, eliminating chronic hunger and extreme poverty.

Is there a vision or understanding of wealth that can inspire transformation of other nations? Why are some nations so poor and others so rich? Why do some have such brilliant and capable people but seem incapable of generating wealth? Do cultural values and beliefs condemn whole cultures to poverty, and lend others to wealth creation?

Most of us don't engage in world-level economics. We just know the resources are limited and demands increase. But "real-world economics" applies to everyone on an everyday basis. We may not all be dealing with empty cupboards, but a business owner knows she has only a *limited* availability of other resources. Personal time and energy only go so far. Her labor force and working capital are restricted. She and her team must decide how best to use those resources to maximize their company's potential. Decisions must be made because of the limitations. But multiply those decisions millions of times a day across the nations of the earth, and "small" choices carry massive impact.

And across the world people are toiling for subsistence and survival. It is easy to see the peasant in Markham's imagination: *"Bowed by the weight of centuries he leans upon his hoe and gazes on the ground, the emptiness of ages in his face, and on his back the burden of the world."*[48]

## Toil's Toll

Something is riding on the backs of humanity. A relentless stick drives us. Elusive promises dangle in front of us like baited hooks to keep us moving blindly forward. It is the tyranny of toil. Leaders are led away by it. Masters are mastered and kings are enslaved. Humanity plods blindly toward some undefined finish line.

It is not supposed to be like this.

Creativity explodes from God's nature. All of creation testifies to the substance of an eternal Creator. Every form, every color, every sound and movement reveal some manifest testimony of the brilliance and loving attention of a creative God. Dive into the microcosm and find an entire universe of beautiful simplicity and stunning complexity. Explore the macrocosm of the heavens and enter mind-blowing expressions of expanse and eternity. Observe creation around us and see stunning symbiotic relationships and design, reminders of a wonderful God with a high value for life and beauty.

When He created all this, God called it good.

Then God formed Adam. With a forceful breath into Adam's body God began an eternal and beautiful call and response of love and praise and laughter. Every life-giving breath from Light brought an exhale from Adam. He was no longer simply dust. Word breathed spirit and purpose into man and his response was worship. "From Him and through Him" came the breath that brought man to life. And "to Him" came the first heart of a man fully alive with words of love and worship. Rising to his feet, hands lifted, I wonder, were his first words "Hallelujah!" or "I love you"? Either way, the call and response of love and delight was awakened.

God inspired every dimension and frequency of Adam's existence imaginable. He took Adam from the wilderness and set him in the Garden of Eden, where Adam's partner, the magnificent woman Eve, was fashioned.

Adam and Eve were pure in heart, undivided in their passions. They were fully in love with God, fully in love with one another. Naked and without shame they would walk together with God through the expansive garden, friends with the Most High.

God gave them dominion over creation, bestowing upon them the authority and power to rule over the earth that they were called to fill. In Psalm 8:5 David marvels that God intended man to be "ruler over the works of Your hands." All the resources were available to them to govern the creation of God. Envision operating at full capacity of body, intellect, and imagination with constant access to the Creator of all things. If they did not have a solution to a problem, they could ask questions and find solutions in their daily evening walk.

David continues by declaring that man was "crowned with glory" (8:5). "Crowned," or *atar* in Hebrew, means "to encircle." It may refer to a crown set upon, or surrounding, the head. But it can also mean something that totally wraps around, such as a shield or strategic clothing that covers, providing protection. The Father's original creation of man included crowning him with glory, completely encircling him with His "radiance, effulgence, weightiness, importance, and wealth."[49] No wonder Adam and Eve were unashamed in their nakedness (Genesis 2:5). They were completely clothed in the glory of God.

But Adam and Eve chose to eat of the fruit of the tree of the knowledge of good and evil in direct disobedience to the command of God. Immediately they recognized their nakedness. The clothing of God's glory was lost to them. Guilt and shame began the insidious drive of humanity into hiddenness and separation from God. They could still talk with God, asking of Him and receiving, but the separation caused by sin broke the intimate fellowship where openness and confidence were commonplace. Pain and suffering became a human condition. Creation grew unruly, fighting against man's purpose to bring order and peace to the heavens and the earth. Man lost the covering of glory, and fulfilling work turned to toil.

Toil is more than the struggle that comes with a difficult task or job. The Hebrews understood toil as a snare, a trap that entangled the prey. The result of toil was always a fight for survival.

These were the deteriorating conditions we inherited. A type of second law of thermodynamics kicked into high gear as every realm of man's existence tended toward chaos and decay. Whether in tending a garden or maintaining relationships or our physical health, everything required a tremendous amount of energy to hold together. The need to "cover our nakedness" through control, success, materialism, and countless other "isms" drives us and consumes every resource we toil to acquire.

Our culture boasts that we are more advanced, more intelligent than humanity has ever been. Yet separation from God has kept us from our fullest potential and capacity for which we were originally created. Eating from the tree of the knowledge of good and evil caused the slow death of every aspect of human life.

Jesus taught His disciples to pray, "Give us this day our daily bread, and deliver us from evil," or "the evil one" (Matthew 6:13). The root of the word "evil" is toil.[50] Toil is a crucial element of the evil one's plot to chain humanity to wickedness. Frustrated, powerless, and purposeless, sinful humanity became addicted to the enemy's solutions. Idolatries like Baal or Asherah worship promised relief from drought and blessing on agriculture—until more sacrifices were required. Humanity set on a quest to escape toil by listening to the demands and empty promises of…Toil.

Things Jesus taught His disciples were revolutionary to humanity and to economics. Through the authority and overcoming power of God, dominion was restored to the second Adam and those born of His Spirit. Toil no longer needed to be the defining fruit of an existence or the driving force of our economy.

## Biblical Worldview

Vishal Mangalwadi, considered by some to be India's foremost Christian scholar, wrote, "The Bible created the modern world of science and learning because it gave us the Creator's vision of what reality is all about."[51] The Bible of the Jewish and Christian faiths provided a blueprint for building Western Civilization. The Bible dominated centuries of shaping Western culture, giving the West its "soul." It taught of one God who is good, who called all creation good, and who valued man and woman. It gave purpose and meaning to creation, value and liberty to all humanity. It inspired creativity and innovation. Its words gave foundation and wisdom for rationality and morality and strengthened and stirred the human heart to compassion. The Bible points the wanderer to a Savior, the suffering to an anchor of hope, and the oppressed to deliverance and freedom from corruption.

Hinduism teaches that the material universe is intrinsically evil. Therefore, detachment from worldly pursuits moves a person closer to salvation. The highest state of being exists in silence and emptiness—

Nirvana. Nothingness is the ultimate reality. If Hinduism is the tree, the fruit of the tree is escapism. Hinduism inspires people to escape the world. Their belief in fatalism results in fear. They exist as victims, powerless against injustice and unrighteousness. Their belief in so many capricious gods promotes eternal insecurity, hoarding, and impoverishment.

The American culture, by contrast, was shaped by a Protestant theology that explained "humanitarian inventiveness, pursuit of wealth, business practices, and commercial success."[52] Consider the most powerful ethical principle in Christianity—love. Most religions separate themselves from the poor, the orphan, or the infirm. Mangalwadi writes, "The hallmark of Indian spirituality was detachment from worldly pursuits like agriculture. Therefore, the spiritually 'advanced' in my country treated the toiling masses as untouchables."[53] As intelligent as the people of India were even in the nineteenth century, creativity and innovation did not extend to making life easier for the poor who worked the fields.

Martin Luther and John Calvin, on the other hand, restored the radical biblical idea that the work of a peasant was as high a calling as that of a priest. Every believer was a saint! God's command to work was unconditional. In the work ethic of American Protestantism, "no one could claim exemption from work on the grounds that he had enough wealth on which to live."

In America in 1850, Cyrus McCormick, a Christian farmer and inventor, believed that his work was a calling from God and that his vocation would be for the glory of God. McCormick invented a reaper that could harvest twenty acres a day. He transformed agriculture and the world.[54] His vision to create industrial machines that could release people from slavery revolutionized the agriculture industry around the world. Ingenuity with equipment could produce far more resource in less time while at the same time freeing people for other valuable pursuits.

God's intention for humanity was to deliver them from toil and the evil behind it. He desired to draw them into a transformational relationship with Himself. He gave promises to Abraham that shifted paradigms for the people of God. Promises of land ownership to a nomadic people transformed their understanding from vagabond wanderers to wealth builders able to be a blessing to all the families of the earth. Their whole economic system was founded on land ownership, a necessary key for capitalism to flourish.

Within a few generations the people of God were slaves in Egypt. None of the Hebrews owned land. They existed under the cruel demands of toil.

God delivered his people out of slavery through Moses. But many found it easier to think like slaves. Someone else made decisions for them. Obey the masters. Be passive. Don't think or take initiative. Slaves submit. Expect to be fed and own nothing. Live in fear. But as Harold Eberle says, "All of these attitudes are contrary to the understanding that people are created in the image of God with the mandate to govern their own lives and steward the earth."[55]

The government of the Hebrews was founded on the Ten Commandments. The first command was to have no other gods and worship the one true God. Reverence Him, even fear Him (Exodus 20:4-7). Eberle uncovers how essential this is for government and economics: "(T)he concept of one God was essential for people to understand and manage this world, but it is also foundational for a successful government and an effective economic system. As Proverbs 9:10 tells us, 'The fear of the Lord is the beginning of wisdom.' Only people who fear God will govern themselves. No amount of governmental control can restrict sin, selfish ambition and rebellion if the people do not first govern themselves. No government or economy will prosper, succeed and continue if God is not at the head."[56] A capitalistic system can propel a nation forward economically, but if that nation does not submit to God, the power of the economic engine will move it in the direction of the hearts of fallen humanity.

The Bible, both Old and New Testament, shapes a culture that sustains an effective economy. The book of Proverbs is filled with parables and wisdom sayings, many of them addressing character in life and economics. A homonym of the word for Proverbs can mean "to rule, to take dominion" or "to reign with power."[57] The following proverbs give a vision of the broad reach in economics found in just one chapter of the Old Testament:

> "Gaining wealth through dishonesty is no gain at all. But honesty brings you a lasting happiness" (Proverbs 10:2, TPT).
>
> "The Lord satisfies the longings of all his lovers, but he withholds from the wicked what their souls crave" (10:3, TPT).
>
> "Slackers will know what it means to be poor while the hard worker becomes wealthy" (10:4, TPT).
>
> "Know the importance of the season you're in and a wise son you will be. But what a waste when an incompetent son sleeps through his day of opportunity!" (10:5, TPT).
>
> "A rich man's wealth becomes like a citadel of strength, but the poverty of the poor leaves their security in shambles" (10:15, TPT).
>
> "The lovers of God earn their wages for a life of righteousness, but the wages of the wicked are squandered on a life of sin" (10:16, TPT).

These are simply a few words of wisdom from just one chapter out of the Bible that help serve as a foundation to capitalism and economics. These are intended to assist the stewards of the economy of God in taking dominion or ruling with power. God intends that Christians experience the truth of His wisdom and apply it to every aspect of His household.

## Fruit Inspection

Jesus taught His disciples that a tree will be known by its fruit (Matthew 7:16). Examine the fruit and you can recognize the quality of the tree, whether religion, philosophy, or economics.

Three primary economic systems operate in world economy: socialism, communism, and capitalism. Let's briefly examine the fruit of each tree.

**Socialism** is a system "advocating collective or governmental ownership and administration of the means of production and distribution of goods."[58] It is a system in which there is no private ownership of business.

**Communism** is a system of production where private property ceases to exist and the people of a society collectively "own" (through the government) the tools of production. Communism does not use a market system, but instead relies on a central planner who organizes production (tells people who will work in what job) and distributes goods and services to consumers based on need.[59] The government uses military strength to impose its will on society. Communism is atheistic and seeks "control over social and cultural life."[60]

Socialism and communism have severely detrimental effects. Oversized and over-controlling government robs people of the reward of their labor, whether it is a physical product or intellectual property. Personal motivation dies. Entrepreneurial creativity and innovation are sacrificed to serve an unwieldy government and a flimsy communal ideal. Socialism also assumes all people will work with the same diligence and character. It is founded on a faulty premise of human nature, that all people are equally wise and good. There is no judging one to be wise, another to be foolish. Individuality is downplayed under the importance of the collective. Government and community provide meaning and purpose. Therefore, creativity and innovation are discouraged. One person must not appear to rise higher than another. Clothing, art, and architecture reflect colorless conformity. In most all socialist endeavors, atheism and humanism rise to oppose religion, particularly Christianity.

**Capitalism** "is an economic system characterized by private or corporate ownership of capital goods, by investments that are determined by private decision, and by prices, production, and the distribution of goods that are determined mainly by competition in a free market."[61]

Capitalism was built originally on the foundation of God's nature and His Word. It affirms the individual, builds family, teaches wisdom in living and stewardship of resource. Capitalism untethered from its anchors in God, moral law, and family will become selfish and oppressive. When people in each mountain of influence re-anchor their hearts in God, the economic system course corrects. Compassion, cooperation, and diversity promote increased productivity and prosperity.

While proponents of socialism chop away at the tree of capitalism, they do so at their own demise. Mangalwadi quotes mid-twentieth-century British author George Orwell, a strong socialist with atheistic leanings. As the atrocities of two World Wars, Fascism, Nazism, and Communism unfolded, Orwell had to face what he saw from these political and economic ideologies. He grieved their fruit, writing of the consequence of the "amputation of the soul": "For two hundred years we had sawed and sawed and sawed at the branch we were sitting on. And in the end, much more suddenly than anyone had foreseen, our efforts were rewarded, and down we came. But unfortunately there had been a little mistake: The thing at the bottom was not a bed of roses after all; it was a cesspool full of barbed wire... It appears that amputation of the soul isn't just a simple surgical job, like having your appendix out. The wound has a tendency to go septic."[62]

After years of championing socialism, George Orwell was foreseeing its tragic fruit. His essay "Notes on the Way" came after reading a book from a noted contemporary of his, journalist Malcolm Muggeridge, *The Thirties*. Muggeridge, an atheist who later came to Jesus after spending time with Mother Teresa in Calcutta, reflected, "(W)e are living in a nightmare precisely *because* we have tried to set up an earthly paradise. We have believed in 'progress.' Trusted to human leadership, rendered unto Caesar the things that are God's... There is no wisdom except in the fear of God; but no one fears God; therefore there is no wisdom. Man's history reduces itself to the rise and fall of material civilizations, one Tower of Babel after another...downwards into abysses which are horrible to contemplate."[63]

Real-world economic realities impact every one of us. Tyranny and injustice exist across the world at the hands of those whose hearts have been snared by an enemy that steals, kills, and destroys. Political and economic systems in the hands of unrighteous rulers perpetrate "amputations of the soul."

But there is good news! As royal sons and daughters of the King of all Kings, we have opportunity to heal those same hearts and bring transformation to the nations. In fact, you have keys of the Kingdom that will lock the door to chronic hunger, disease, and poverty. The same keys can unlock resources and provide for the masses.

Keys like seven loaves of barley and a few small fish.

# 11

## Wealth Transfer and Kingdom Advancement

*It was winter and the deck chairs were put away. Small piles of snow sheltered in corners of the deck out of reach of the snow shovel. I looked out the window toward the blanketed city and the horizon to the west. I felt a longing within me. Something was stirring. I asked the Father, "Would You show me more of Your Kingdom in my city and land?"*

*Immediately, I saw Holy Spirit walking at my side along a road in my city. He was carrying several buckets of paint. I could feel His excitement; His pace was quicker than usual, like we were about to engage in a bit of holy mischief! I sensed I was about to see things that had been invisible to me until now.*

*Holy Spirit began splashing paint of every imaginable color. This was not a sprinkling of paint from a brush. He launched bucket after bucket at the unperceivable places in my city. He passed me a couple of cans, one with vivid blue, the other an amazing deep red. I launched them and immediately doubled over in laughter! The joy of creating with Holy Spirit was indescribable. The paint began to reveal outlines and eventually entire structures I had never seen before. Beautiful and magnificent buildings appeared that took my breath away. Somehow, they were ancient and future at the same time. They were immovable and seemed as though they would last forever. But they also looked flexible and dynamic, able to grow and adapt.*

*These buildings were inconceivable in value. I could focus on a section of a wall or foundation and zoom in on light-bending gems; gold and silver were tessellated into the design with brilliant craftsmanship. These structures were futuristic and seemed to defy physics.*

*Every uniquely crafted building was completely at peace in its environment. It was as if each structure knew the design and destiny the Creator had given the land. The masterpieces were in unity with their surroundings.*

*The more Holy Spirit splashed paint on my city, the more structures were revealed. I saw that the materials of the buildings were emanating light. It was natural to be drawn to them. My eyes became clearer and I began looking with more focus and intent, understanding I was seeing things of eternal substance in my territory.*

*As Holy Spirit was leading me along the streets in this spontaneous party, I realized the experience was changing the way I walked. I was more confident and intentional, less tentative. I became aware that others saw the way I was walking. Some were curious. Others were critical, even angry. Apparently, I was walking with Holy Spirit in places marked on their maps as "out of bounds" and "dangerous," even "evil." But I had no desire to engage their criticism. I was having too much fun painting the town with the Spirit of God!*

*As I pondered this experience later, these ancient-future foundations and buildings revealed a reality far deeper and greater than I had ever seen. They were alive, inextricably connected to the King of the Kingdom, Jesus. They exuded His life and beauty. It was as if God financed a massive city revitalization project, assigning His best architects, builders, and innovators to make this entire city an invitation to eternity.*

## God Has a Plan

God is building a beautiful House on earth. His Kingdom is complete in heaven, but much of it has yet to be built on earth. Building the

Kingdom is the essence of transformation. We, the Ekklesia, are building powerful structures that exude light and life, a place of habitation for the Living God, not just a resort for Him to visit. The house of God is being built street by street, business by business, city by city.

Transformation requires wealth. Just because it is God's Kingdom does not mean it will not cost anything. Through the prophet Haggai God made it clear to the remnant gathering in Jerusalem that rebuilding the house of God would incur costs. He reminded His people that the foundations for the temple had been set, but nothing had been done for sixteen years. Meanwhile, the people worked on their own houses. Consequently, finances dried up for their own projects, and there was nothing left for God's plans. God made it clear they were facing the fruit of their decision to withhold their tithe from Him. Without obedience from His people, God's plans for His house could not be accomplished.

A generation of prophetic voices in the Church have been declaring with boldness that which the prophets of old proclaimed: the people of God will receive massive wealth. "(T)he wealth on the seas will be brought to you, to you the riches of the nations will come.... Your gates will always stand open, they will never be shut, day or night, so that men may bring you the wealth of the nations—"; "You will feed on the wealth of nations, and in their riches you will boast" (Isaiah 60:5,11; 61:6).

Peter Wagner said, "God is poised to release enormous, unprecedented amounts of wealth for the advancement of His Kingdom here on earth."[64] God is ultimately the source of this release of unprecedented wealth. "The Lord will grant you abundant prosperity...in the land he swore to your ancestors to give you" (Deuteronomy 28:11).

The Ekklesia is intended to receive and steward this wealth for the purposes of the Kingdom of God on earth. But many Christians have a vague impression of how this happens. They imagine it looks something like this: The struggling Christian launches a prayer for finances. Suddenly, an unbeliever feels compelled to give the pious, praying

Christian all her wealth. The Christian goes on a shopping spree, and the great wealth transfer is somehow "complete."

The word "transfer" may be confusing by the way some groups choose to interpret this prospering of the church. It gives the impression that all the church must do is wait passively, and the wicked will line up to unload their ships of wealth into the bank accounts of the righteous. There will be a shifting of wealth to the righteous for many reasons, but to see it as the "wicked" throwing all their money at the righteous, who sit passively, praying for fat bank accounts, may reap only disappointment.

This great wealth transfer has eternal purpose, more than simple comfort or passive, self-centered, luxurious living. It is focused on the commission to baptize and make disciples of all *nations*, teaching them to observe the commands of Jesus. The sons and daughters of the King are resolute to build the Kingdom as God builds the Church.

How *does* this transfer come to the Church? It comes to the Ekklesia, first, supernaturally. It is miraculous provision fulfilled by God. Like when my pastor friend walked into a hospital in Mozambique with a bag of food and *everybody* was fed. The wealth transfer can even come through unbelievers responding in gratitude for what God has done for them or their families. It is released, secondly, by wealth repossession (the returning to believers of the wealth that previously had been lost or stolen). The wealth transfer comes, thirdly, through wealth creation by the Church. Kingdom people create value in services and goods for which people are willing to pay a premium price. Empowered stewards in the Kingdom become wealth creators, and they attract wealth creators *into* the Kingdom of God.

The great transfer of wealth is going to happen. How do leaders of the house of God prepare for this shift and steward the resources to fulfill our Father's plans and advance His Kingdom?

## Wealth and How to Generate It

Wealth is more than money. Look up dictionary definitions, however, and it is difficult to discern a difference. The English word "wealth" originated from a now obsolete word, "weal." Weal refers to "a sound, healthy, or prosperous state: Wellbeing."[65] As Pastor Sunday Adelaja says, "The original meaning of wealth was: 'to possess great qualities, values and virtues.'"[66]

Wealth is about prospering even as our souls prosper in all areas of life in the Kingdom of God and in relationship with Him (3 John 2). God has plans for us, including to prosper us (Jeremiah 29:11). Prosperity as understood by Hebrews has the sense of meaning "to be led along a good road." "I am the Lord your God, who teaches you what is best for you, who directs you in the way you should go" (Isaiah 48:17). This includes every aspect of life, from character, relationships, and internal life, to material blessings like land and finances.

Deuteronomy 8:17-18 speaks of God's intent for His people: "You may say to yourself, 'My power and the strength of my hands have produced this wealth for me.' But remember the Lord your God, for it is he who gives you the ability to produce wealth, and so confirms his covenant, which he swore to your forefathers, as it is today." In Christ, we have access to God's wisdom, favor, grace (empowerment), and ability to create wealth. Any true wealth comes as result of covenant relationship with God, not simply by our own effort and resourcefulness.

True wealth is actively pursuing and possessing the fullness of God's resources through relationship with Jesus Christ. Therefore, "righteousness is true wealth, for it is the possession of God's character."[67] True wealth of righteousness opens a way for financial resource.

If true wealth is both intangible and tangible, how does a person generate wealth? It begins and flourishes in a genuine relationship with Jesus, for "from Him, through Him, and to Him are all things."

Relationship releases the faith, the fear of the Lord, and the character transformation necessary to give us the ability to truly build wealth. (See Isaiah 33:6.) Practically, there are several important steps to generating wealth:

1. Tithing (give generously to God, Who gives all things generously to us)
2. Paying Yourself (saving and investing)
3. Self-discipline (cutting superfluous spending)
4. Wealth Mindset (using money as seed to generate more)
5. Mindset of the Steward (stewarding God's economy/house with wise planning)
6. Godly Partnerships (seeking advice from proven stewards of resource)
7. Generosity (giving to others as Holy Spirit leads)

The intent of financial wealth is to invest resource in that which will provide returns (dividends, interest, etc.). The return either becomes a resource for living expenses or reinvested for multiplication. The foundational resource continues to earn additional interest, hopefully outperforming the constant drain of inflation.

Chief Stewards look for a return on investment. They seek to increase and multiply what is entrusted to them, their capital. We have all heard the adage, "Don't just give a man a fish; teach him *how* to fish." Harold Eberle says that God taught the Hebrews one step beyond: own the pond where people fish.[68] Faithful stewards do more than give away loaves of bread. They plant seed and harvest, train bakers and build bread factories.

# Why Hasn't the Church Seen the Great Transfer of Wealth?

Several obstacles stand in the way of most of the Church receiving this transfer of wealth. One of the primary powers opposing the transfer is the spirit of poverty.

This is more than a mindset that can be counseled and shifted. The spirit of poverty is a demonic spiritual power that works fiercely against the Ekklesia and the Kingdom. God's plan to prosper the Church is necessary both to demonstrate the truth of God's covenant with His people as well as to provide for the massive transformation of the nations.

Yet the spirit of poverty has strong influences on the Church, disrupting both the covenant inheritance and transformation of the nations. It deceives the people of God and keeps the church in impoverishment.

*Resistance to prosperity.* Christians influenced by the spirit of poverty react negatively to teaching on prosperity. Resistance to prosperity puts up a wall barricading against the release of provision for the very things for which many leaders and churches are praying. Ironically, this includes the Great Wealth Transfer. Granted there are some teachers of a prosperity theology who are influenced more by greed than generosity. But that does not invalidate a true theology of prosperity.

*Driven by fear.* The spirit of fear partners with the spirit of poverty. Fear is a target-forming spirit. Fear of lack targets the believer for insufficiency. Fear of theft seems to unleash the thief. Poverty is a curse, and fear works as a driver, keeping the Church from accessing the faith necessary to access God's provision and treasures. Fear acts as a veil, blinding people to the protection of God on their behalf. As a result, God's people are fearful of stepping out, taking risks, walking by faith. They choose to walk in the "certainty" of what they can see with the eyes of their flesh rather than the eyes of faith.

*Blinded to options.* The spirit of poverty removes the believer's ability to see options, thus removing a significant capacity to be creative. I teach students in our classes on creativity and innovation that creativity is defined by having multiple options. Poverty curtails creativity. It is a brutal limiting of options. As wealth in the soul soars through our royal identity as sons and daughters of God, options begin to multiply, opening us to the possibilities God has set before us.

*Passivity* is a side effect to poverty. It can look like a Christian resigning themselves to the status quo. "If God wanted me to do this, He would have given me the money to do it." Or it can look like an entitlement mindset, waiting passively for the "blessing" to drop out of heaven like winning the Christian lottery. The steward actively pursues options and solutions.

*Living for sufficiency.* As a lid, the spirit of poverty may cause a Christian to concede that God provides, but His provision is *just enough* to get them through the challenges. Like the leader preaching that "My grace is sufficient for you" means that God gives *just enough* provision to meet our need—not less, and certainly not more. This limitation of grace and provision incites a constant battle between two Christian values: 1. *Be content in every situation* versus 2. *Be generous on every occasion.* It begs the question: how can one be generous to others when there is barely enough to provide for one's own current needs?

*Escapism.* Another factor keeping the Church impoverished is a theology of escapism prevalent in much of the Church. For many, the prevailing Christian forecast is darkness and more darkness, heading to certain doom and destruction. The purpose of God, they suppose, is to remove us from this realm before He destroys it. In which case, provision is not a significant priority or need. Plans stretching twenty years into the future seem pointless, let alone plans for a thousand years.

## Preparation for Wealth Transfer

In our cities and nations, what steps can we take for apostolic provision and advancement of the Kingdom of God? Whether you steward a local

WEALTH TRANSFER AND KINGDOM ADVANCEMENT

or regional church, a shop on Main Street, or a movie production studio, you can prepare for the transfer of wealth for Kingdom advancement.

**Apostolic Alignment:** Align yourself and your organization with an apostle. Apostles and prophets provide a spiritual authority and power that bring your group into life-giving relationships. Apostolic centers provide more than accountability and education, though both are important. They provide a strong family relationship with a connection to Father's plans for a region or nation. There is also an increase in flow of grace and anointing. When my wife and I brought our church back into an apostolic relationship with Che and Sue Ahn, and Mark and Ann Tubbs of Harvest International Ministries, we immediately felt the family connection. The protection and empowerment we felt amid a season of intense spiritual warfare was real. We also experienced an immediate lift in favor and finances.

Because there is a vast worldwide vision, a massive amount of provision is necessary. But the provision cannot be fully released without the proper alignment designed by God. Alignment with the fivefold ministries, as revealed in Ephesians 4, restores wisdom and integrity that can be trusted with such resources. This is especially true of the ministries of the apostles and prophets. Because these two ministry gifts are responsible for laying strong foundations, they are graced with power and authority to set things in order. They build the church with strength to bear the weight of the provision necessary to fulfill its purpose.

Apostles and prophets carry a high level of authority in their assigned territories to pull down spiritual strongholds, allowing the release of vision and provision within the body of Christ. But the functioning of all fivefold ministries is vital for the transformation of the Seven Mountains of Influence. The release of prosperity comes in alignment, and it comes in agreeing with God.

**Value What God Values:** In our world people operate under a variety of competing value systems. Situational ethics erodes away Christian morality, with millions of people wandering on countless pathways declaring, "*My* truth." But the Bible is clear in teaching that which God values. Paul instructs the Ephesian Christians to live as children of light and "find out what pleases the Lord" (5:10). "Without faith it is impossible to please God," we learn in Hebrews (11:6). "And whatever you do," Paul says, "whether in word or deed, do it all in the name of the Lord Jesus, giving thanks to God the Father through him" (Colossians 3:17). As we seek His heart, our hearts become pliable. Our values are influenced by the impress of His signature ring upon our nature, infusing His character and purpose into our identity. What pleases Him pleases us. His passions become our passions.

**Be Generous:** Because He is generous, we can be generous on every occasion. Because He withholds nothing from us, we withhold nothing from Him. We see the value of the tithe, the first fruits, and the alms.

Generosity wages war against the strongholds of poverty. Lisa and I were in a season of transition and financial need, feeling oppression in our city. We helped host a conference for the churches in our community on breaking the cycle of poverty with James Ryle. At the end of the event, the leaders received an offering specifically to break the stronghold of poverty. Holy Spirit challenged Lisa and me with an amount we knew was a faith adventure. We gave joyfully. Within a week we had the inspiration and opportunity to begin a small business. Not only did we have personal financial breakthrough, but the atmosphere shifted in our city. Even the price of fuel began coming down to prices consistent with our region.

**Discipline:** God values integrity, just scales, and obedience. If I were giving a million dollars to someone, I would want to see wisdom demonstrated in their character. Do they have integrity? Are they principled in the spending of resource? Do they have vision for it that will cause it to reproduce? Are they driven by needs, or led by the Spirit? Do they have a plan for *more than* a million dollars? These conditions of character and behavior require discipline.

**Build:** The chief steward has an attitude toward increase. Burying the assets in the backyard is pointless. Their desire is to look toward harvest! How can we build now that will maximize the coming harvest? Their mindset is on producing value in the King's economy, not hoarding resource.

A mature son and daughter steward prophetic words, and the Father's economy is established in the realm of our measure of rule. Prophecies provide excellent building material with which we can build the Kingdom.

As our family was "sheltering in place" during the 2020 COVID-19 incident, we considered what God was saying and doing in this puzzling season. We pulled out our collection of prophetic words gathered since 1994. As we read through these powerful words, we discovered tools for building and insight into our corporate destiny. Because we have prophetic confirmations of our destinies and callings over the years, we were able to persevere through opposition and discouragement. It also gave us the power and insight to know how to build in the new season.

Compile your own Book of Destiny. Establish a collection of all the meaningful, prophetic words, visions, and dreams given to you over the years. Read them out loud. Pray them, ponder them, and dream with God.

We build out of revelation. It is tempting to build a business out of our knowledge, or structure a family based on our childhood training, or fashion a church out of a past revival or someone else's formula. We need revelation from the heart of the Father and the mind of Christ.

We saw earlier that God established a pattern in the Old Testament that chief stewards need to understand: Word + Spirit leads to God's Order, which leads to Glory. Begin with revelation, and the Word and Spirit set everything into God's order, bringing glory to God.

As a son or daughter stewarding a rich inheritance, you have been given a vision to build. The economy that you are building will function best by constructing the following into your Kingdom enterprise:

**Power Plants**— Power generation is essential for development and growth. Activate and train an intercession team. They will be the Power Plant of your business or ministry. Without prayer we are unable to grow in health. This is our "war room," the place where we hear the strategies of God for our ministry or business.

Intercession teams are necessary for clearing the land and atmosphere for prosperity and wealth generation. Over the years the enemy has sought to lock up wealth, making it inaccessible to the Church and Kingdom ministries. Apostles and prophets working together with intercessors can cleanse the land of defilements that lock up resources. They engage in identificational repentance for such sins as idolatry, greed, sexual impurity, boundary moving, shedding of blood, and God-robbing. Ongoing cleansing and spiritual maintenance of the region allow for a breakthrough of both vision and provision for the Kingdom churches in a region.

**Worship** is a core part of the atmospheric development in a region. It has the power to shift the attitudes and perspectives in the region as you release the sounds of worship and praise into air. Thanksgiving crushes the oppression of grumbling and negativity. Intimacy with God through worship opens access to the lavish resources of heaven for generous distribution.

When a land has been cleansed, worship teams are necessary to fill the void. Work with worship leaders to encourage consistent worship besides just Sundays. As the sound of the region shifts toward praise and worship, a strong atmosphere for the Kingdom is developed. His stronghold is established, providing protection for believers and the wealth necessary to bring forth His vision for the region.

**Spiritual Engagement Initiatives.** Worship will bring clarity of revelation for strategic advancement. Identificational repentance and strategic warfare prayer will provide traction toward the purposes of God in your church, city, and region. Use the keys of the Kingdom to close doors that allow the enemy to access your business, school, or ministry. Then open doors that Holy Spirit is showing you to release His purposes.

Jesus taught us to *plunder the enemy's house* (Matthew 12:22-29). "Who would dare enter the house of a mighty man and steal his property? First, he must be overpowered and tied up by one who is stronger than he. Then his entire house can be plundered, and every possession stolen. So join with me, for if you're not on my side you are against me. And if you refuse to help me gather the spoils, you are making things worse" (12:29-30, TPT).

**Shift the Church Culture.** Develop a healthy culture for prosperity within the church by teaching biblical principles for prosperity and wealth. Provide practical classes on money, finances, and Kingdom business. As chief stewards we model this to our people, providing permission for them to dream and envision more for the future, pulling on the resources of heaven to activate the dreams. Train people in their identity as royal sons and daughters and as stewards of the resources of God.

For example, a Christian business was undercharging and practically giving their services away out of their sincere desire to serve God and bless people. But it was critically affecting their financial bottom line. They were constantly under stress for finances. It was robbing resources from the owner's family, and they had little else to sow into the Kingdom. Their church began to teach on Kingdom foundations for life and business. When the business aligned itself with biblical teaching, they began to draw appropriate boundaries. They saw the value of their services and product and began charging prices commensurate to that high value. Their own needs were met, and they were able to be generous to those in need. They began to sow more into Kingdom vision. Before long they had expanded into new areas of business, and their positive influence began to encourage other businesses. A culture was beginning to shift.

**Vision and Goals.** Leaders will attract wealth when they have a vision for the Kingdom. Without vision for the ministry, there will be no demand for provision. It is also necessary to set goals that will allow the leaders and ministry to stay on track for productivity. A study of Harvard

MBA graduates revealed that those who set financial and career goals before graduation made ten times the income of those who had no goals. This is an important step for leaders of Kingdom ministries in shifting the church culture from sufficient living to abundant ministry.

**Church Finances.** An effective church or ministry will prepare itself for strong wealth attraction by putting in place a strong wealth-management plan. In addition to normal, healthy fiscal practices, the church could develop an IRS-approved organization, similar to a foundation, that can be set up to provide dividends to the church. A separate board would be set up with specific parameters given for investment guidelines, dividend instructions, and board responsibilities. People could be encouraged to give to this fund, like a gift to a foundation. The principal of this fund would remain to earn interest, but the dividends could be used by the church or ministry expense.

The intent of this practice would be to grow the fund to an extent where the dividends could fund an increasing percentage of the practical expenses of the church. Meanwhile, more and more of the tithe given would be freed up to go toward the vision and expansion of ministries for the church and beyond. Continued growth of these investment funds would provide a healthy financial prospectus for the church and ministry.

As business and government leaders in the community begin to see the health and wisdom of the church, more trust will be developed within the community. Businesspeople will become more willing to give and invest in the ministry as they see wise use of resources. With these strategies in place, more wealth will be handled by the church for the blessing of the city and the building of the Kingdom.

Meanwhile, as the church begins to shift its culture, the pastors and leaders can begin to meet with other pastors and leaders, encouraging them and expanding the vision of handling prosperity for the Kingdom of God. As this becomes adopted by more churches, a region will become heavily influenced by the wisdom of wealth management in the Kingdom of God, further attracting the favor of both God and man.

## The Great Transfer of Wealth

God intends for us to walk in His favor as His sons and daughters. We are responsible to mature, just as we expect any child to grow. Handling the resources of God is a very practical and necessary growth development needed within the Body of Christ. As we manage what we have been given with wisdom, we are entrusted with more. As we position ourselves for true prosperity, we learn how to effectively grow that wealth in a way that gives testimony to the greatness of God.

Our small business was growing. It was 2005 and I was learning how to manage the growth pains of transitioning from a family business to hiring employees. I walked into the bank to talk with the vice president about opening a line of credit for our business after two years of operation. He looked over our profit and loss statements. Impressed by the financial bottom line, he asked me, "What did you do prior to starting this business?"

"I pastored churches."

With my admission, he launched into a ten-minute diatribe on how horrible churches, and especially pastors, are with money. Forgetting our success, he ranted about irresponsible use of funds and lack of transparency. He spewed about poor financial and business planning and embezzlement. He clearly had a lot to bluster about. To that businessman, pastors and churches had little integrity and respect for financial health and success, which he knew to be crucial to being productive members of a community. I couldn't help thinking that the banker did not see the irony of his comments!

But I knew his stories had merit. I had seen much of it in my years on the church mountain. With each stab I felt the sting of reproach upon the church, and ultimately on God. But as this businessman ranted with the passion of an Old Testament prophet, I realized I was sitting in a divine appointment.

The banker finally reengaged the decision before him, congratulated us on a successful business, and sent me out with approval for a line of credit. I received much more than financial stop gaps that morning. I realized the wind of Holy Spirit was moving me in a completely different realm of revelation—the unveiling of the economy of heaven released on earth.

Every believer in Christ, especially leaders, needs desperately to hear the cry of this banker. How can we manage the economic treasures of heaven if we do not manage earthly resource? How can we tolerate continuing with a terrible reputation in handling money? "They're horrible with money. And then they want more handouts!" he had said. It is not hard to assume that they question whether we are like our God. Does the Almighty care only about "heavenly stuff" and neglect the practical, rubber-meets-the-road kind of issues people face every day? Does He reward impoverished thinking and have it out for those who seek to be wealthy and successful?

God has a long-range plan that was launched at the beginning of time. "And because of God's unfailing purpose, this detailed plan will reign supreme through every period of time until the fulfillment of all the ages finally reaches its climax—when God makes all things new in all of heaven and earth through Jesus Christ" (Ephesians 1:10, TPT). You have a crucial place in God's plan. He gave you a destiny, that you would "fulfill the plan of God who always accomplishes every purpose and plan in his heart" (v. 11, TPT).

God intends that we access heaven's resources to accomplish His Kingdom purposes on earth. "His divine power has given us everything we need for life and godliness through our knowledge of Him," Peter reminds us (II Peter 1:3). Access the power and provision of heaven's economy. The great transfer of wealth is progressing, and the Kingdom of God is advancing.

# 12

## Living in Heaven on Earth

Stewards are impact leaders on the earth. They release Kingdom authority and resources with every decision they make. The "Acts of the Apostles 2.0" is being released in our day. A massive invasion by the Kingdom of God is rising upon the landscape of the nations of the earth. Jesus refused to take a shortcut to receiving his inheritance—the bride and the nations of the earth. Now we, the Bride of the Lamb, are poised to release the Kingdom of God into the nations, offering them to the King.

Kingdom stewards, as administrators of the economy of God, operate with vision and strategy. God has a vision for His house, His business. Jehovah-Jireh has a perfect strategy for market saturation and product dominance. And He has chosen to share His power, authority, and unlimited resources—in fact, Himself—with His hand-picked, world-class stewards, the children of God.

Therefore, as stewards of the Kingdom we have vision for the future, with dreams to pull heaven into earth's realm. We have access to every strategy of God to exercise dominion and authority in the areas to which He has called us. Every resource is available to us for transformation, from personal development to the stewardship of nations. The hidden things of God are being revealed to his people, an inheritance intended to be enjoyed forever (see Deuteronomy 29:29).

As we receive the impress of His character on our lives, our desires resonate with the frequencies of heaven. Doors in heaven and earth begin to unlock before us. And we begin to see what we have believed: Nothing is impossible for God.

Suppose a community of the Ekklesia began to operate as chief stewards in the House of God. What if they took Kingdom Economics as a challenge, a magnificent adventure, and a treasure hunt? What could it look like? What if they saw heaven as a brilliant warehouse of all the promises and resources of God waiting to be brought to earth? And what if they knew they have the authority and power to transfer those treasures to earth, transforming cities and nations? I suppose we would see His glory manifest as never before.

## The Power of Expectation

"The creation waits in eager expectation for the sons of God to be revealed" (Romans 8:19).

Expectation is a powerful force. In the Kingdom of God, expectation is born out of faith, hope, and love. Anticipation is strengthened and launched when the Ekklesia joins in thanksgiving and praise. "And the news about Him spread throughout the surrounding area... when the sun was setting, the people brought to Jesus all who had various kinds of sickness, and laying His hands on each one, He healed them" (Luke 4:37, 40).

Counterfeit expectation placed in what the kingdom of darkness provides, on the other hand, emerges out of unbelief and hopelessness. Add a generous chorus of grumbling and complaining, and the atmosphere becomes toxic. Strong, negative expectation hangs all around, sucking hope out of the atmosphere. We get what we expect. "And they took offense at Him... He could not do any miracles there, except lay His hands on a few sick people and heal them. And He was amazed at their lack of faith" (Mark 6:3, 5-6).

A black swan event is an unpredictable occurrence in economics. It is rare but it carries severe impact. When COVID-19 hit the world in 2020 and the subsequent economic crisis, the force of fear and severe pessimism far surpassed the effect of the pandemic. Every culture-shaping mountain pushed hard with expectation for the worst possible outcomes. Evil was on a feeding frenzy with racism, riots, accusations, and oppression of liberties. Many in the church hid in their proverbial storm cellars, cowering in fear and uncertainty. Panic was more contagious than the disease they feared.

However, the expectation of a mature steward is not based on economic indicators, headlines in newspapers, or decisions made in the halls of government. Our hope is grounded in God and His economy. We look to His word and prophecy for our news and instruction. Even when we are squeezed by the enemy's intimidation tactics, our eyes are lifted to the Father and our voices are filled with praise. Faith, hope, and love outlast the crisis and overpower the voices of doom.

How strong is your expectation? One of us can cause a thousand stormtroopers of the enemy to run away, and two of us intimidate ten thousand. No longer do we cave in when just one person in the office is grumpy. Our encounter with a negative clerk having a bad day no longer ends up becoming our bad day. In fact, we shift the atmosphere. Our expectation for glory is stronger than the world's pessimism. We carry the "atmospheric pressure" of heaven, and we expect that glory is going to dominate the emotional and spiritual weather scene.

Expectation is a foundation for Kingdom impact. The assurance we carry as Kingdom sons and daughters has power to transform families, workplaces, even cities and nations. We have come to know God as the One who lifts our heads. We have strength in our hope-muscles because we seek first the Kingdom of God and His righteousness. And now we anticipate taking back territory, as we exercise our dominion with the King.

## Maximum Kingdom Impact

Living in the Kingdom of God changes everything. As sons and daughters of God, we are learning to live in a radical standard of excellence. We maintain a vision of extraordinary provision and performance in every realm of our lives. We are men and women of integrity, focus, and resolve, whose flex is feared by hell, even while we laugh and enjoy life! We pursue massive atmospheric and economic transformation. Economists of the House of God are living and managing our resources with an expectation of maximum Kingdom impact.

Transformation is demonstrable and measurable, not theoretical. Economic transformation in the Kingdom of God is no exception. George Bernard Shaw, author and satirist, wrote, "If all the economists were laid end to end, they'd never reach a conclusion" (Shaw, n.d.). As the Holy Spirit moves upon the Ekklesia in this season, we will reach more than a conclusion. We will contribute to transformation of the nations.

What is your expectation? Take practical steps toward transformation as you develop apostolic stewardship in God's economy. Expect maximum Kingdom impact as you:

1. **Dream Big:** The previous caretaker, our enemy, has utilized poverty and fear to quench dreams and vision, assuring compliance to its diabolical agenda. Many of us have thrown the wind of our dreams to the savagery of caution. Without vision, people perish. As a leader you have a powerful purpose story. Where you come from and your successes and failures and hardships provide a landscape where dreams and vision and goals rise like giant landmarks. That big dream is not just for you. Peter Senge said, "Without a genuine sense of common vision and values there is nothing to motivate people beyond self-interest."[69] Search out people in your office or church who want to be part of something bigger than themselves. Get in the presence of

LIVING IN HEAVEN ON EARTH

God. Dream big, take more risks, and build something important together.

2. **Be Sincere**: Since God has made it possible for us to have sincere and open access to Him, operate in the same sincerity with the people around you. Your business or ministry will experience greater freedom and increased productivity. Many organizations are corrupted with internal politics and gameplaying. "Political" leaders, whether in business or church or government, believe that people are motivated by self-interest. So they dangle promises of power and wealth in front of them, but control and manipulate from behind the curtain. Because we operate in the realm of God's mercy and grace, our organizations empower people to operate openly and honestly. Imagine the impact worldwide if the tangled web of bribery no longer existed.

3. **Engage in Meaningful Communication**: Dialogue is more than a discussion between you and me. Broken into its two components, *dia* means "through," and *logue* is "word, or meaning." It could essentially be translated "meaning passing through." A dialogue is like a stream flowing *between* us; not *from* me to you, or you to me. You and I are two banks with a river of meaning, purposeful language and thought, moving downstream through us to other people. Toxic dialogue destroys everyone who is downstream. But life-giving dialogue sows seed and awakens fruitfulness in people in our organization who are downstream from us.

4. **Create Value**: People are hungry and desperate for Kingdom goods and services. You have authority and power to distribute the resources God has given you. A business entrepreneur creates value by starting a business. They provide income for others and desirable products that improve people's lives. Some industries are more in the business of *extracting* value than creating it. (Read John Bogle's book *Enough* and his warning to the financial and banking industries concerning their practice of

value extraction.)[70] The Ekklesia must not underestimate the influence and power potential in releasing even the simplest of heaven's treasures.

5. **Exercise Apostolic Authority**: Chuck Pierce observes, "Apostolic authority must be established in a field if we are to reap the harvest of that field."[71] Apostles are necessary to take the lid off the land that is locking up the resource. God has a design for your territory and an authority structure to unlock it. If you are not aware of who the apostles are in your region, pray for revelation, and pray they be raised up together with the prophets. Operate within the apostolic structure. Define your own metron. Access the resources God has imbedded in the assignment to accomplish the commission.

6. **Become a Learning Organization**: Whether you are a ministry organization, media, or business, Kingdom-minded leaders go beyond being sponges of new information. The economy of God flourishes because those who distribute the resources of heaven operate in new thinking, or *metanoia*. The church interprets *metanoia* as "repentance." And it usually comes packed with a strong expectation of sorrow. Generations of condemnation in preaching and teaching have caused a tentative nature in many Christians who have been in the church long. But *metanoia* also means a "shift of mind." In other words, "have another thought." Generate creativity. Become innovative. Business has become the locus of innovation in our world. It is time that Kingdom stewards on every mountain exercise their divine imaginations and become the pioneers and architects who change the world.[72]

7. **Use the Keys**: Remember, you have the *keys of* the Kingdom, and using these keys gives you access *to* places in the House of God that the enemy currently controls. Keys lock up anything that is a hindrance to God's purpose. Keys also unlock supply needed to advance God's purposes. Apostles and prophets carry

keys that are necessary to unlock the Kingdom of God in a region, but all of us possess keys within our measure of rule that have the potential to unlock a cascading download of Kingdom vision and provision, unlocking divinely appointed destinies.

8.  **Assemble the Team:** Apostolic teams are relevant and necessary for every mountain of influence. Just as Jesus spent the night praying before He appointed the twelve apostles, you should get revelation from Father. These men and women will be stewarding the vast economy of God. They are called to walk in maturity in fivefold giftings according to Ephesians 4. I encourage you to equip them with *The Five Fingers of God: Discovering Your Destiny Through the Fivefold Gifts* by Mark Tubbs. This resource provides the clearest and most effective pathway to maturity and operation in the fivefold gifts of any that I have read. This team will operate more like a family at mealtime rather than a stark, rigid board following "Robert's Rules of Order." Structure is necessary, but relationships are foundational. An excellent resource for assembling apostolic teams is *Apostolic Governance in the 21ˢᵗ Century: How to Build a World-Class Apostolic Center.* Greg Wallace, an apostolic administrator, has done a brilliant job communicating essential building blocks and steps necessary for building a team and an effective apostolic center.

9.  **Develop Credibility:** Chris Fussell was part of developing a new hybrid of leadership in the war in Iraq. The idea was to communicate the "One Mission" to every person engaged in battle. As each soldier owned the mission, leaders emphasized the following formula for building successful teams to accomplish their mission: Credibility = Proven Competence + Integrity + Relationships.[73] Place this as a tool in the hands of the chief stewards in your metron. As Christian leaders in every mountain practice this, not only will credibility be restored to the Church and the Kingdom, but effectiveness and productivity will far

exceed anything the enemy has done in the past. Determine your organization's One Mission, communicate it, and develop a Kingdom force that establishes credibility within the field of your assignment.

## Supernatural Economics

God is releasing new authority for this season in the earth. Leaders with the impress of the King are being raised up and commissioned into assignments prepared by the Father from the foundation of the earth. A new level of holiness is emerging in God's people. It is not defined merely by an absence of flesh and self-focus but rather by the substance of God's holy nature radiating from the midst of them.

New strategies for victory are being released. Leaders access their keys with greater confidence and authority, and enemy forces are being exposed and defeated. The warriors are on the move and restoring the Father's estate to its intended glory. They are facilitating a transference of power to gain wealth so that Kingdom purpose and destiny can be fulfilled.

With divine wisdom, these chief stewards are becoming decisive. They are cutting off all other options but one—Father's plan. As wise stewards, they know when it is time to set up camp for training, resting, and increasing combat skills. Or when it is time to advance, engage the mission, and possess the land. They operate in the knowledge that they have the power to get wealth, even before the battle is won and the spoils of war are accessible.

Expect supernatural miracles to happen as you step into your identity, authority, and power as a son or daughter of the King. Be a bold distributor of every resource you have been given, with the knowledge that God is able to multiply what you offer in faith. You will discover the economic principle of *koinonia* exploding grace-gifts in every street of your city as you share your portion outside the four walls of a church.

Miracles will increase faith in you and those around you. The faith boost will begin to release supernatural supply to accomplish the mission you have been assigned. As you give wise stewardship to the resources that spring up around you, everything you need will be accessible to achieve God's purposes.

Anyone can see darkness getting darker. We have heard enough of the doom and gloom sermons and the coffee shop rants. Death has won too many battles. Poverty and humiliation have choked and destroyed millions. Sickness, addictions, and injustice mock humanity with the indignity of darkness. Wars, greed, and lust steal from us and brutally bankrupt any sense of value we hope to possess.

Have your eyes open, Ekklesia. The brightness of His dawn is bursting in power around us. His greatness is towering over the enemy and its pathetic works. The Kingdom of God is increasing from glory to glory. And in the light of His glory, heavenly treasures are hanging heavy, like ripe fruit just waiting for us to pick. This is our inheritance. It is everything we need for life and godliness.

Are you ready for God to ignite your heart and imagination? Holy Spirit has come to light a fire in us, making us so heavenly minded that creation's groans become sighs of contentment. The sons of God are waking up. The bride is stirring with a dreamy glimpse of her bridegroom. Stewards in the Ekklesia are accessing the economy of heaven, and the House of God is prospering. Just when darkness releases its piercing attempts to drain the body of Christ of its hope and lifeblood, the dread champions of the King are rising with the strength and resource of the Risen One.

Arise, Ekklesia. The Economy of God is being released in power.

*"Who has ever given to God, that God should repay him?*
*For from Him and through Him and to Him are all things.*
*To Him be the glory forever! Amen."*

# Bibliography

Adelaja, S. (2016). *Money Won't Make You Rich: God's Priciples for True Wealth, Prosperity, and Success.* Milton Keynes, UK: Golden Pen Limited.

Amadeo, K. (2019, June 25). *2007 Financial Crisis Explanation, Causes, and Timeline.* Retrieved from thebalance.com: www.thebalance.com/2007-financial-crisis-overview-3306138

Ariely, D. (2009). *Predictably Irrational: the Hidden Forces that Shape Our Decisions.* New York: Harper Collins Publishers.

Bauer, W. (1979). *A Greek-English Lexicon of the New Testament* (Fourth ed.). (W. F. Gingrich, Trans.) Chicago: University of Chicago Press.

Bogle, J. C. (2009). *Enough. True Measures of Money, business, and Life.* Hoboken, NJ: John Wiley and Sons, Inc.

Boller, M. a. (2016, May 13). *3.4 Gracelets.* Retrieved from Contemplative activist.com: contemplative-activist.com/2016/05/13/3-4-gracelets/

Burke, P. (2003, Autumn). *Carmelite Spirituality – Poverty.* Retrieved from Carmelite web site: http://www.carmelites.ie/poverty.html

Campolo, T. (1981). Speech at Northwest Nazarene College, unpublished. Nampa, Idaho, USA.

Chappelow, J. (June, 29 2019). *Economics: Overview, Types, and Economic Indicators.* Retrieved from Investopedia: https://www.investopedia.com/terms/e/economics.asp

Chuck D. Pierce, R. W. (2001). *The future War of the Church.* Ventura, CA: Regal Books—Gospel Light.

Creighton, J. (2016, January 17). *The Largest Galaxy in the Known Universe*. Retrieved from Futurism: https://futurism.com/ic-1101-the-largest-galaxy-ever-found

Dubay, T. (1989). *Fire Within*. San Francisco: Ignatius Press.

Duewel, W. L. (1989). *Ablaze for God*. Grand Rapids, Michigan: Zondervan.

Eberle, H. (2010). *Compassionate Capitalism: A Judeo-Christian Value*. Yakima, WA, USA: Worldcast Publishing.

Engle, L. (1998). *Digging the Wells of Revival*. Shippensburg, PA: Destiny Image.

Femirite, T. (2011). *Invading the Seven Mountains with Intercession*. Lake Mary, Florida: Creation House.

Fussell, C. (2017). *One Mission: How Leaders Build a Team of Teams*. New York: Penguin Random.

Goodyear, C. F. (2017). *One Mission: How Leaders Build a Team of Teams*. New York: Portfolio/Penguin.

Griffin, W. (2015-2017, January 1). *Gracelets: Being Conduits of the Extravagant Acts of God's Grace*. Woodinville, WA, CA, USA: Harmon Press.

*Hebrew-Greek Key Word Study Bible New International Version*. (1996). Chattanooga, TN: AMG Publishers.

Ken Blanchard, P. H. (2016). *Lead like Jesus revisited: lessons from the greates leadership role model of all time*. Nashvill, TN: W Publishing.

Kierkegaard, S. (n.d.). *114 Insightful Quotes from Soren Kierkegaard*. Retrieved from The Famous People: https://quotes.thefamouspeople.com/soren-kierkegaard-212.php

Kittel, G., & Friedrich, G. T. (1985). *Theological Dictionary of the New Testament*. Grand Rapids: William B. Eerdmans Publishing.

Kluth, B. (2020, July 31). *Small Town, Small Church, Small Salary.* Retrieved from National Association of Evangelicals: www.nae.net/small-town-small-church-small-salary

Lewis, C. S. (2014). *Christian Reflections.* New York: Harper One Publishers.

Mangalwadi, V. (2011). *The Book That Made Your World: How the Bible Created the Soul of Western Civilization.* Nashville: Thomas Nelson.

Markham, E. (n.d.). *The Man With the Hoe.* Retrieved July 25, 2020, from Poets.org: https://poets.org/poem/man-hoe

McCarthy, N. (2020, May 7). *COVID-19 Wreaks Economic Havoc Across Europe (Infographic).* Retrieved from Forbes: https://www.forbes.com/sites/niallmccarthy/2020/05/07/covid-19-wreaks-economic-havoc-across-europe-infographic/#47fd2eb0521a

McCollam, D. (2009, March). Limitless Possibilities Conference at The Mission. *Sermon.* Vacaville, CA, USA.

McKenzie, R. (2020, July). *Jesus and Economic Life.* Retrieved from Kingwatch: http://kingwatch.co.nz/Christian_Political_Economy/jesus_and_economic_life.htm

McLeod, S. A. (2020, March 20). *Maslow's hierarchy of needs.* . Retrieved from Simply Psychology.: https://www.simplypsychology.org/maslow.html

*Merriam Webster Dictionary capitalism.* (n.d.). Retrieved from Merriam Webster Dictionary: www.merriam-webster/dictionary/capitalism

*Merriam-Webster interdict.* (2020). Retrieved from Merriam-Webster Dictionary: www.merriamwebster.dictionary/interdict

*Merriam-Webster socialism.* (n.d.). Retrieved from Merriam-Webster Dictionary: www.merriam-webster.com/dictionary/socialism

Munroe, M. (2006). *Kingdom Principles: Preparing for Kingdom Experience and Expansion*. Shippensburg, PA: Destiny Image Publishers.

*New American Standard Bible*. (1960, 1962, 1963, 1968, 1971, 1972, 1973, 1975, 1977). La Habra, CA: Thomas Nelson Publishers.

Nikolovska, H. (2020, December 22). *30 Church Giving Statistics and Facts*. Retrieved from Balancing Everything: https://balancingeverything.com/church-giving-statistics/

Pass, C. (2002, 2005). *Collins Dictionary of Business, 3rd ed*. New York: Harper Collins Publishers.

*Poverty Rate by Country 2020*. (2020, April 1). Retrieved from World Population Review: www.worldpopulationreview.com/countries/poverty-rate-by-country/

Rowe, C. (2017, July 19). *The Borgen Project*. Retrieved from Causes of Poverty in Haiti: https://borgenproject.org/causes-of-poverty-in-haiti/

Ryle, J. (n. d.). Grace! Grace! Grace! The Fullness of God's Empowering Presence. Longmont, Colorado: EnVision Ministries.

Senge, P. M. (1990). *The Fifth Discipline: The Art and Practice of the Learning Organization*. New York: Doubleday Currency.

Shaw, G. B. (n.d.). *George Bernard Shaw Quotes*. Retrieved May 12, 2020, from BrainyQuote.com: https://www.brainyquote.com/quotes/george_bernard_shaw_105433

Silvoso, E. (2014, 2017). *Ekklesia: Rediscovering God's Instrument for Global Transformation*. Grand Rapids : Chosen Books.

Sorge, B. (2000). *Glory: When Heaven Invades Earth*. Grandview, MO: Oasis House.

Spake, K. (2012). Apostolic authority: differences between power and authority. In B. Cook, *Aligning with the apostolic: as anthology of apostleship, volume 2* (pp. 151-166). Lakebay, WA: Kingdom House Publishing.

Spencer, A. B. (2014). *2 Timothy and Titus: A New Covenant Commentary*. (M. F. Keener, Ed.) Eugene, OR: Cascade Books.

Taylor, J. (2016, October 10). *The Conversion of Charles Finney*. Retrieved from The Gospel Coalition: https://www.thegospelcoalition.org/blogs/evangelical-history/the-conversion-of-charles-finney/

Tenny, T. (1999). *"God's Favorite House"*. Shippensburg, PA: Destiny Imiage.

*The Greek New Testament, Third Edition*. (1966, 1968, 1975). New York: American Bible Society.

*The Holy Bible, New International Version*. (2002). Grand Rapids, Michigan: Zondervan.

*The Passion Translation*. (2017). Broadstreet Publishing Group.

Thomas Cooley, P. R. (2020, June 5). *A Quick Turnaround in Employment*. Retrieved from U.S. Economic Snapshot: https://www.econsnapshot.com/

Uys, J. (Director). (1980). *The Gods Must Be Crazy* [Motion Picture].

Vallotton, K. (2018). *Poverty, Riches, and Wealth*. Bloomington, Minnesota: Chosen Books.

Wagner, C. P. (2015). *The Great Transfer of Wealth: Financial Release for Advancing God's Kingdom*. New Kensington, PA, United States of America: Whitakerhouse.

Wagner, P. (2012). *On Earth as it is in Heaven: Answer God's Call to Transform the World*. Bloomington, Minnesota: Chosen Books.

Wallace, G. (Ed.). (2019). *My Father's Business: Discipling Nations.* Pasadena: Wagner University.

*weal.* (2019). Retrieved from Merriam Webster: http://merriam-webster.com

William F. Arndt, F. W. (1957, 1979). *A Greek-english Lexicon of the New Testament and other Early Christian Literature, 2nd edition.* Chicago and London: The University of Chicago Press.

# Endnotes

1   Wallace, "My Father's Business."
2   Nikolovska, "30 Church Giving Facts."
3   Kluth, "Small Town, Small Church."
4   Markham, "The Man with the Hoe."
5   Matthew 28:19-20.
6   Femirite, "Invading the Seven Mountains."
7   Spencer, "2 Timothy and Titus," 117.
8   McLeod, "Maslow's hierarchy of needs."
9   Uys, "The Gods Must Be Crazy."
10  Munroe, "Kingdom Principles," 31.
11  Duewel, "Ablaze for God," 28.
12  Dubay, "Fire Within," 312.
13  Sorge, "Glory: When Heaven Invades Earth."
14  "Hebrew-Greek Key Word."
15  "Hebrew-Greek Key Word."
16  "Hebrew-Greek Key Word."
17  "Hebrew-Greek Key Word."
18  Creighton, "The Largest Galaxy."
19  Tenny, "God's Favorite House."
20  Campolo, unpublished speech.
21  Kittel & Friedrich, "Theological Dictionary," 828-829.
22  Kittel & Friedrich, "Theological Dictionary," 186-191.
23  McCollam, Limitless Possibilities Conference.
24  Vallotton, "Poverty, Riches, and Wealth," 145.
25  Ryle, "Grace, Grace, Grace."
26  "Hebrew-Greek Key Word," 1686.
27  Griffin, "Gracelets."
28  "Hebrew-Greek Key Word," 1644.
29  "Hebrew-Greek Key Word," 1606.
30  "Hebrew-Greek Key Word," 1655.
31  Kittel & Friedrich, "Theological Dictionary," 901.
32  Kittel & Friedrich, "Theological Dictionary," 590-591.
33  Ariely, "Predictably Irrational," 23-25.
34  Kittel & Friedrich, "Theological Dictionary," 447-450.

35  Lewis, "Christian Reflections," 33.
36  Arndt, "A Greek-English Lexicon."
37  Engle, "Wells of Revival."
38  Merriam-Webster Dictionary.
39  Bauer, "A Greek-English Lexicon," 876.
40  Kierkegaard, "114 Insightful Quotes from Soren Kierkegaard."
41  Ken Blanchard, "Lead Like Jesus Revisited," xiii.
42  Spake, "Apostolic Authority," 154.
43  McKenzie, "Jesus and Economic Life."
44  Thomas Cooley, "A Quick Turnaround in Employment."
45  McCarthy, "COVID-19 Wreaks Economic Havoc."
46  "Poverty Rate by Country 2020."
47  Silvoso, "Ekklesia," 36.
48  Markham, "The Man with the Hoe."
49  "Hebrew-Greek Key Word," 1610.
50  Kittel & Friedrich, "Theological Dictionary," 912-914.
51  Mangalwadi, "The Book That Made Your World," xxi.
52  Mangalwadi, "The Book That Made Your World," 317.
53  Mangalwadi, "The Book That Made Your World," 318.
54  Mangalwadi, "The Book That Made Your World," 315-316, 319.
55  Eberle, "Compassionate Capitalism," Loc 177 of 2011.
56  Eberle, "Compassionate Capitalism," Loc 197-198 of 2011.
57  "The Passion Translation," 202.
58  "Merriam-Webster Dictionary."
59  Chappelow, "Economics: Overview."
60  Eberle, "Compassionate Capitalism," loc 983 of 2011.
61  "Merriam-Webster Dictionary."
62  Mangalwadi, "The Book That Made Your World," 3.
63  Mangalwadi, "The Book That Made Your World," 23.
64  Wagner, "The Great Transfer of Wealth," loc 600 of 2602.
65  "Merriam-Webster Dictionary."
66  Adelaja, "Money Won't Make You Rich," 19.
67  Adelaja, "Money Won't Make You Rich," 66.
68  Eberle, "Compassionate Capitalism," loc 437 of 2011.
69  Senge, "The Fifth Discipline," 274.
70  Bogle, "Enough."
71  Pierce, "The Future War of the Church," 162.
72  Senge, "The Fifth Discipline," 13-15.
73  Fussell, "One Mission," 17.

CPSIA information can be obtained
at www.ICGtesting.com
Printed in the USA
LVHW010326160621
690355LV00015B/641